LOVE FOOD
Love Paris

Author: Kate Whiteman

Manager World Travel Guides: Connie Austen-Smith

Managing Editor: Katey Mackenzie

Senior Editor: Sandy Draper

Senior Designer: Carole Philp

Page Design: Alison Fenton

Picture Research: Liz Boyd and Liz Allen

Copy-editor: Hilaire Walden

Proof-readers: Lesley Levene and Ruth Baldwin

Index: Hilary Bird

Cartography: Geoff Chapman

Map Illustration: Chapel Design & Marketing Ltd

Produced by AA Publishing

© Automobile Association Developments Ltd 2006

ISBN: 0-7495-4913-0

ISBN-13: 978-0-7495-4913-8

Published by AA Publishing (a trading name of Automobile Association
Developments Limited, whose registered office is Fanum House,
Basing View, Basingstoke RG21 4EA; registered number 1878835).

A02730

The contents of this book are believed correct at the time of printing.
Nevertheless, the publishers cannot be held responsible for any errors or
omissions or for changes in the details given in this book or for the
consequences of any reliance on the information provided by the same.
This does not affect your statutory rights.

When following recipes, it is advisable to use all metric, imperial or cups
measurements not a mixture.

Colour separation by MRM Graphics Ltd, Winslow, Buckinghamshire
Printed in China by C & C Offset Printing Co. Ltd

The AA's website address is www.theAA.com/travel

LOVE FOOD
Love Paris

BOULEVARD PERIPHERIQUE

MONTMARTRE

SACRÉ
COEUR

PARC DE LA
VILLETTE

① Gare
du Nord

Gare
St-Lazare

Gare
de l'Est

BOIS DE
BOLOGNE

ARC DE
TRIOMPHE

AVENUE DE CHAMPS-ÉLYSÉES

②

PLACE DE LA
CONCORDE

③

JARDIN DU
TUILIERIES

④ PALAIS DU
LOUVRE

PLACE DE LA
RÉPUBLIQUE

⑤

CENTRE GEORGES
POMPIDOU

Seine

NOTRE-
DAME

⑥

PLACE DE LA
BASTILLE

TOUR
EIFFEL

⑦ HÔTEL DES
INVALIDES

MUSÉE
D'ORSAY

⑧

PALAIS DU
LUXEMBOURG

Gare
de Lyon

Gare
Montparnasse

PANTHÉON

Gare
d'Austerlitz

⑨

BOULEVARD PERIPHERIQUE

Seine

Contents

Recipe Contents

Welcome to Paris

In this most romantic of cities, the passion for food is as all-encompassing as the passion for l'amour. Parisians devote as much care to choosing, cooking, and eating food as they do to nurturing a romance. It is almost impossible to think of Paris without thinking of food.

And what variety! Unlike the French regions, Paris has no particular cuisine of its own. As the capital, it has never needed to develop one, since the best chefs from every region and foreign country have always converged on the city, bringing their own specialties with them. So you won't find many places serving "typically Parisian" dishes, but you will find authentic local dishes from every region of France and every corner of the globe, from Alsace to Zanzibar.

It's no surprise to discover that the world's first restaurant was in Paris. Until 1765, the only places to have a meal were at home, or at an inn, where drink took precedence over food, and meals were a pot-luck affair served on the whim of the innkeeper. All that changed when Monsieur Boulanger (who may or may not have been a baker) opened a shop in what is now the rue du Louvre, advertising *restaurants* — "restorative" broths. These thin medicinal slops were the only cooked food he was legally allowed to sell because he was not a member of the closed-shop traiteurs' union. One day, however, he offered a thick stew-like soup of sheep's feet in white sauce. The union sued him for breaching their monopoly, but the redoubtable Boulanger won his case and the right to sell solid food. He was quick to capitalize on his victory and started to offer a range of dishes for diners to choose from a menu; the world's first restaurant was born. The Parisians took to the idea with gusto and a restaurant boom began.

Over the next two centuries, Paris clung on to its enviable reputation as the haute cuisine capital of the world, home to glamorous temples of gastronomy serving sophisticated dishes rooted in classical French techniques. Nowhere else on earth could you find such luxurious ingredients, unctuously sauced, or such showy presentation served by supercilious waiters, in such elegant surroundings. But as chefs vied to outdo each other, high-class restaurant cooking became ever more contrived, with increasingly arty and elaborate presentation (remember the excesses of nouvelle cuisine?), which eventually became more important than the food itself. By the millennium, Parisians and visitors had begun to rebel against over-priced, over-elaborate cooking which ignored global influences, and a revolutionary force of young chefs stormed in to modernize and diversify the restaurant scene, stirring in a soupçon of exoticism with ladlefuls of flair. Inspired by this new wave of innovative cooks, the old guard was forced to rethink.

Legendary Michelin three-star chefs like Alain Senderens, Alain Ducasse, and Joël Robuchon abandoned outmoded formality in favor of congeniality; they opened affordable bistros and stylish tapas-style bars, and updated their classic dishes with fresh inspiration and subtle spicing. Restaurants have acquired a new buzz and appeal and Paris is now one of the most exciting places to eat in the world.

For Parisians, eating out is a way of life. It is quite common for working couples to dine out almost every night at their favorite *cantine*, a modest local eatery where the food is unfailingly decent if not spectacular, the welcome warm, and prices low. In every quarter I asked local residents where they shopped for food, and in each neighborhood I met at least two or three women who said they rarely cooked at home; it is so much easier and just as cheap to go to the local bistro. If they do make supper chez elles, they pick up a ready-prepared dish from the traiteur or the late-night supermarket, and never make a dessert. What's the point when their local fromagerie offers a huge selection of perfectly ripe cheeses, and the neighborhood pâtisserie sells an array of fabulous desserts?

Whatever your mood or budget, you can be sure of finding a restaurant that's right for you in Paris. But with the menus in the windows often looking much the same, it can be difficult to know which to choose from the plethora of bistros, brasseries, restaurants, and cafés. As a rule of thumb, a bistro is a small neighborhood establishment, often family-run, with a cozy atmosphere and a handwritten blackboard menu offering homely dishes. Many old-established Paris bistros have hardly changed in a hundred years. They look like parodies of themselves, with yellowing lace curtains at the window, dingy paintwork, and plain wooden tables (sometimes shared with other diners), but the inauspicious ambience is no indication that the food won't be good. It certainly won't be haute cuisine, but a good bistro will offer trencherman's portions of good-value, home-cooked dishes — perhaps a coarse terrine with country bread and cornichons (the dish is left on the table for you to help yourself), then coq au vin, kidneys or rabbit in mustard sauce, chocolate mousse or a home-made tart — all washed down with a carafe of rustic table wine. Traditional bistros still adhere to formal opening times (usually

12.30–2pm for lunch and 7–11pm for dinner), closing in between, so you can't pop in whenever hunger pangs strike. Because they are family-run, many also close at weekends and take long vacations in August.

For all-day (and sometimes all-night) eating, your best bet is a brasserie. Although they originated in Alsace as bars serving beer (brasserie means "brewery") and local dishes like choucroûte and charcuterie, brasseries have evolved into the paradigm of Parisian eating. At any time of day or night in a popular brasserie you'll find a cross-section of Parisians: lovers lingering over breakfast or seductively swallowing succulent oysters for supper; gaggles of workers piling into platters of steaming sausage-crowned choucroûte; or solitary diners enjoying the plat du jour. (Except in the grandest restaurants, Paris is a comfortable place to dine alone.) Waiters in long black aprons bustle about, holding aloft trays laden with drinks or iodine-scented plâteaux de fruits de mer, although in some places, the lively atmosphere and art nouveau décor can outshine the food on your plate. For sheer exuberance and a true taste of Paris, you can't beat iconic establishments like La Coupole and Bofinger, where foie gras and spanking-fresh seafood star alongside the choucroûte in fabulous belle-époque surroundings. For food lovers, these brasseries are unmissable attractions; some are even classified as protected national monuments alongside the Louvre and the Eiffel Tower.

As for restaurants — they come in myriad guises, ranging from *hors catégorie* ("unclassifiable") gourmet establishments, offering unutterable luxury at unthinkable prices, to the ubiquitous fast-food joints. However, you can still enjoy a perfectly

acceptable steak at the Hippopotamus and Quick (pronounced "Queek") chains, and *moules-frites* (mussels and fries) at Léon de Bruxelles — far better than the usual fast-food fare. Like bistros, restaurants usually have rigid opening hours for lunch and dinner. You'll be lucky to be served lunch after 2pm or dinner after 11pm, although most of the large chains are open all hours.

A trip to Paris would be unthinkable without a visit to one of its 10,000-plus cafés. Café culture is an essential part of life here. Parisians spend hours in cafés enjoying a drink, reading the newspaper or a book, gossiping with friends, putting the world to rights, and, most important, people-watching. For locals, it's perfectly acceptable to spend several hours over a single cup of coffee; on fine days, tourists are likely to be hustled out by when disorderly queues form to grab a vacant pavement table. Café food is generally basic at best, but eating is not the point; the fun is to sit outside or on the terrace in the hope that a friend or neighbor will pass by and join you for a chat. You only have to watch impossibly fashionable young people or fur-swathed old ladies displaying like peacocks to realize that cafés are for seeing and being seen. Cafés range from seedy, smoke-filled *zincs*, with battered zinc counters, to *philo-cafés* where latter-day philosophers gather to emulate Jean-Paul Sartre and his cronies, exchanging ideas over a glass of absinthe, to glamorous designer salons and famous tourist traps, where a single coffee costs as much as a full meal. Each has its own particular ambience and charm, so wherever you find yourself, pull up a wicker chair at a round zinc-topped table and do as the Parisians do — drink in the atmosphere of the city.

11

Parisians are passionate about food, whether they eat out or at home. Inevitably, the proliferation of supermarkets has changed the way that many shop and eat, but daily food shopping is still an integral part of life. No self-respecting Parisian would buy bread to eat the next day or the day after; it's taken for granted that they will queue up at least once a day for a fresh baguette, warm and fragrant from the oven. Seasonality and regionality are twin obsessions, so they would rather wait for the first juicy strawberries, earthy wild mushrooms, baby eels, or fresh cheeses from mountain regions than buy flavorless produce from far-flung continents.

One of the city's culinary delights is shopping for food in specialty shops and markets. Every neighborhood market has a unique personality and flavor that reflect the character and lifestyle of the locals. It's a joy to arrive at daybreak when the once-or-twice-weekly *marché volant* (roving market) traders arrive to set up their stands overflowing with colorful heaps of fruit and vegetables, cheeses and seafood, poultry and meat. A swift trawl through the stalls will tell you all you need to know about the area's demographics. The immaculate displays of prime produce in the classy Marché Président Wilson indicate understated wealth and gentility. In startling contrast, Belleville market pulsates with the raucous sounds, colors, and smells of Africa. For a few hours, the aromas of spit-roasting chickens, herbs, spices, and pungent cheeses pervade the streets, attracting shoppers who come to sniff and prod before buying, to gossip, and to exchange badinage and recipes with the merchants. By lunchtime, the stalls are gone; the only evidence that the market was there are some broken crates and trampled vegetable rejects for the cleaning department to sweep away. Tomorrow, the traders will be in another part of town.

On non-market days, locals flock to the *rues commerçantes* (market streets), pedestrianized cobbled streets where food shops of every variety spill out exuberantly into the road. Parisians are fiercely proud of their neighborhood shops, which offer everything a gourmet could desire six days a week. Of course it takes longer to potter from the boulangerie to the charcuterie than to dash round a supermarket, but for Parisians it's an enjoyable and indispensable ritual.

So enjoy Paris — undoubtedly the greatest gastronomic city in the world — and its manifold delights of good food and l'amour.

Gare du Nord, Gare de l'Est & Montmartre

(9th, 10th & 18th arrondissements)

Most travelers arriving at the Gare du Nord make a dash for the station exit to join the taxi queue or catch the metro in search of Paris's famous sights. But those who take time to stop and look up will be rewarded by a view of the station's neo-classical facade topped with a row of twenty-three imposing statues, each representing the cities originally served by the station when it opened in 1864. The huge facade of the Gare de l'Est (opposite), which opened in 1849 is equally impressive. Streets in the neighborhood recall the destinations of the first trains, with names such as boulevard de Strasbourg and rue d'Alsace.

Gare du Nord, Gare de l'Est & Montmartre
(9th, 10th & 18th arrondissements)

Across the road from the Gare du Nord, you'll see the quintessentially Parisian Terminus Nord brasserie, with its covered terrace and seafood banc piled high with *fruits de mer*. But turn left into the grimy rue du Faubourg St-Denis and you'll find yourself in another continent. Ignore the prostitutes and pimps lurking in doorways and wander into the souk-like covered passages, where you'll join a throng of busy women in colorful saris crowding the spice markets and Indian emporia of Paris's Little India. If you crave the best food from the Indian sub-continent that Paris can offer, head for passage Brady, with its plethora of cheap, authentic restaurants.

At the southern end of the Faubourg St-Denis, the Indian community is joined by others from Turkey, Africa, and the Caribbean. Ethnic shops from every continent line the warren of covered passages, like the passage du Désir (passage of Desire), something of a misnomer, as many of the buildings are derelict and slightly sinister.

For a flavor of Africa, Barbès market in the nearby 18th arrondissement offers an authentic multi-cultural experience, with crowds jostling through a jumble of colorful clothes, housewares, brightly colored fabrics, ethnic rugs, and anything you would find in a souk. The pervading aroma of exotic spices, bread, and meat grilling on braziers is overwhelming, and the exuberant sounds and colors transport you away from Paris and into exotic Arab and African worlds. The atmosphere is wonderfully heady and exciting, but it's essential to be on your guard and beware of pickpockets.

For a complete contrast, head toward the Gare de l'Est, with its magnificent nineteenth-century architecture, the sole surviving reminder of the railways in their heyday, when trains arrived from Strasbourg laden with precious cargoes of foie gras. There's another belle-époque relic on the corner of rue Chabrol and boulevard de Magenta, the Marché St-Quentin, one of the few remaining original cast-iron and glass-covered markets in Paris. It's a great place to stock up with fresh produce and groceries, particularly if you are boarding the Eurostar.

If you are intent on seeing the sights, walk northward and upward to Montmartre. The hilltop village and the Basilique du Sacré Coeur are must-see spots for any visitor and, naturally enough, the immediate vicinity is a teeming tourist trap. But wander a short way from the fourteenth-century place du Tertre, with its overpriced restaurants, caricaturists, and pushy artists selling lurid landscapes, and you'll find a quiet village with cobbled streets, charming cottages with minuscule gardens tumbling down the hillside, and peaceful squares whose beauty inspired the great Parisian impressionist painters. The squares are delightfully inviting places for a picnic; buy baguettes and fillings in the rue des Abbesses or rue Lepic, then work up an appetite climbing the steep *butte* (hill) and eat your lunch while watching today's artists at work. Who knows? You may even be the first to spot a new Utrillo in the making. If a picnic doesn't appeal, it's still worth exploring the streets at the bottom of the butte for their lively cafés (much less expensive than those at the top) and arty shops and galleries.

In the tranquility of the winding back streets, you can imagine Montmartre as the rural community it once was. Surprising visual reminders remain: the famous vineyard overlooking the cemetery, once tended by

Benedictine monks, and a couple of windmills in rue Lepic (now transformed into busy restaurants), the only ones left of the thirty or so that were once used to press the grapes from the vineyard, and to grind the grain from neighboring villages into flour.

Montmartre also supplied the city of Paris with gypsum (plaster of Paris) that was quarried from the butte in such vast quantities that the hill almost collapsed in the nineteenth century. At the bottom of the winding rue Lepic is place Blanche, which takes its name from the clouds of white dust that rose from the carts carrying wheat chaff and flour from the windmills to the city.

By 1850, the gypsum quarries had closed down and Montmartre became absorbed into the city of Paris. Within thirty years, the farming community had also vanished and been replaced by artists including Corot, Delacroix, Géricault, Degas, Renoir, Cézanne, Manet, Van Gogh, and Toulouse-Lautrec, who found inspiration in the cafés, bars, and louche nightclubs that they frequented, and depicted the bohemian atmosphere of Montmartre in their work.

The legendary cabarets attracted racy female entertainers like Mistinguett and La Goulue, who were immortalized by Toulouse-Lautrec. Nowadays, Montmartre's nightlife is less raunchy, but tourists still congregate on the butte every night to experience a taste of its bohemian past.

Shops in Gare du Nord, Gare de l'Est & Montmartre

Hédiard

If you haven't got much time before catching the train, don't despair. Once you have passed through the international Eurostar check-in at the Gare du Nord, you can still buy a picnic or some edible souvenirs of Paris. The station branch of the luxury gourmet grocer Hédiard doesn't exude the same delicious aroma of tea, coffee, vanilla, and spices of its more glamorously located counterparts but it still sells a large range of pre-packaged pâtés, pickles, and cheeses. It also stocks a reasonable selection of wines. It doesn't sell corkscrews, but will open a bottle of wine for you and supply you with plastic cups for your journey.
GARE DU NORD

Arnaud Lahrer

Colorful china echoes the pink-frosted éclairs and dazzling cakes displayed in the window of this artisan pâtisserie. Raspberry gâteau is particularly tempting, but so are the home-made ice creams, small pastries, fruit tarts, strawberry-and-lichee-flavored *bonheurs* (small cakes).
53 RUE CAULINCOURT, 01 42 57 68 08

Barbès market

You'll find every kind of ethnic food at this heaving twice-weekly market (Wednesdays and Saturdays), which is the focus for Paris's Arab and French-speaking African population. Prices are low, but it's acceptable to bargain for exotic fruits and vegetables, spices, freshly grilled breads, and pastries dripping with honey and nuts. The surrounding streets are packed with halal butchers and cheap ethnic restaurants.
BOULEVARD DE LA CHAPELLE AND BOULEVARD ROCHECHOUART

La Bonne Fournée

Be prepared to queue at this popular neighborhood bakery, where excellent value fresh bread and delicious pastries come hot from the ovens twice a day and are snapped up by eager locals.
151 QUAI DE VALMY, 01 42 05 43 83

La Boucherie Nouvelle

A mounted stag's head on the wall of this high class butcher's indicates that it specializes in furred and feathered game, which is beautifully displayed. Partridges, pheasants, woodcock, and rabbits are piled high in glass

Paul

This small branch of the famous bakery chain is handily located just before the Eurostar boarding entrances. You can buy a freshly baked flûte, baguette, or pain de campagne to take home, or generously filled baguettes to eat on the train. Ask for a delicious savory tartlet to be heated up sur place (the salmon and spinach is particularly good) and there's usually a decent selection of pastries to tempt your tastebuds. If you are taking a train, it's wise to buy your purchases well before you start boarding, as the most popular items sell out fast.
GARE DU NORD

cabinets. If you love eating game, it's impossible not to be attracted by the birds in all their feathered glory. All the meat here is of the highest quality.
13 RUE DU POTEAU, 01 42 23 84 83

Caves des Abbesses

The owner of this attractive wine shop is passionate about his wines and will happily help you to choose the right bottle. There's a small bar at the back of the shop, where you can enjoy a dégustation of cheeses and charcuterie with a glass of wine.
43 RUE DES ABBESSES, 01 42 52 81 54

Charcuterie de Montmartre

This lovely octagonal shop is a treasure trove of some of the finest charcuterie you'll find in Paris. Colorful *compôte de lapin* (rabbit terrine studded with carrots) and rolled chicken breast with fresh morels are joined by fishy creations such as ballotines, terrines, and flavorsome seafood salads. It's all wonderfully fresh and appetizing.
11 RUE DU POTEAU, 01 46 06 36 31

Coquelicot boulangerie/bistro

Artisan baker Thierry sells an extraordinary array of breads at this tiny boulangerie-cum-bistro. Each day brings a different selection of specialty breads like *pain au lard et aux oignons* (bacon and onion), *chèvre et raisins* (goats' cheese and raisin), or *ananas et violette* (pineapple and violet). There's a handy leaflet to advise which bread goes best with what. Lunchtimes bring generously filled sandwiches and baguettes, with fillings that include chocolate and strawberry.
24 RUE DES ABBESSES, 01 46 06 18 77

Epicerie Velan

This is a fabulous bazaar-like store with sacks spilling out rice and dried pulses, spices, chutneys, and all things Indian and Pakistani. Bottles of rose water and sticks of incense add a fragrant note.
83–87 PASSAGE BRADY, 01 42 46 06 06

Godiva

The shop is crammed with tempting boxes of chocolates, many beautifully packaged and ideal for a last-minute present, or to assuage hunger pangs if you are taking a train.
GARE DU NORD

Les Halles de Montmartre

A huge corner greengrocer, with stalls spilling out on to the rue Duhesme. In season, you'll find wild mushrooms along with the freshest fruit and vegetables.
15 RUE DU POTEAU

Marché St-Quentin

One of the few remaining Victor Baltard nineteenth-century "pavilions" complete with a green cast-iron fountain, one of fifty fountains donated to poor areas by the English francophile Richard Wallace, in 1840. The covered food market is a mass of color and life, particularly at weekends, when it's open Saturday morning and afternoon, but only Sunday morning. There's every kind of food on offer in the maze of corridors, from fruit and vegetables to meat, fish, and a great selection of cheeses and charcuterie. If the weight of your purchases gets too much for you, you can stop for some refreshment at the café counter in the middle.
BOULEVARD MAGENTA

Shops in Gare du Nord, Gare de l'Est & Montmartre

Du Pain et des Idées

An old fashioned bakery whose window display is enough to lure you in. Everything is baked in a wood-fired oven, from breads to apple *chaussons* (turnovers), made from halved apples encased in the lightest puff pastry. The pains au chocolat are irresistible to even the most dedicated dieter.

34 RUE YVES TOUDIC, 01 42 40 44 52

Les Rôtisseries de Maitre Guillaume

The delectable aroma of roasting poultry and meat lures you to the rôtisserie, which is full of surprises. Alongside the free-range chickens, you'll find stuffed rabbit, quail, and Cornish game hen (guinea fowl). You can also buy *boudins blancs* (smooth sausages made of white meat) and quail stuffed with foie gras to cook at home.

10 RUE DU POTEAU, 01 46 06 78 57

Sarl Velan Stores

If you feel like cooking an Indian-inspired dish after eating in one of the Indian restaurants that line this crumbling and dilapidated alley, come here for a selection of every kind of spice, chutney, curry paste, and Indian produce you can imagine. Curry lovers will be in heaven as the aromatic scents of garlic, cardamom, and turmeric engulf them.

87 PASSAGE BRADY, 01 42 46 06 06

Pages 20–1: the leafy, cobbled streets of Montmartre are filled with traditional shops, while its picturesque café-lined squares and sweeping panoramas entice you to explore.

Fromagerie de Montmartre

Part of the famous Quatrehomme fromagerie chain. It is almost impossible to walk past the extraordinary array of cheeses in this attractive old shop without being tempted inside to buy at least one perfectly matured specimen. All the cheeses on sale are made using farm-fresh raw milk and are sourced from all over France. There are mountains of fresh butter, crêpes, and wonderful breads to go with the cheeses. Everything is in perfect condition and there's always a selection of seasonal cheeses like brie de Meaux *aux noix* (with walnuts), which has been produced in Paris since the eighteenth century.

9 RUE DU POTEAU, 01 46 06 26 03

Restaurants in Gare du Nord, Gare de l'Est & Montmartre

Moulin Rouge

For traditional glitz and glamor, complete with a hundred dancers bedecked in feathers and rhinestones and performing the can-can, you can't do better than spend an evening at the Féerie extravaganza at the Moulin Rouge. The dancing is faultless, the sets gloriously tacky, and there's a promise of reintroducing the famous underwater tank filled with snakes. If the thought of it doesn't put you off your food, you'll find that dinner, under the guidance of head chef Laurent Tarridec, includes luxurious items like seafood, foie gras, and caviar. The spectacular cabaret and lavish food provide a memorable, albeit expensive, evening out.
82 BOULEVARD DE CLICHY,
01 53 09 82 82

Café Burq

A new chef has transformed the menu at this immensely trendy café-bar with its minimalist 1970s décor and huge picture windows offering a fabulous view of Montmartre. Classic dishes such as *magret de canard* (boneless duck breast) are enhanced with exotic spices, while roast salmon is given a Spanish treatment with chorizo and black olives. Desserts are equally delicious and the music is great, if noisy. Service can be chaotic, so don't go if you are in a hurry.
6 RUE BURQ, 01 42 52 81 27

Chez Casimir

Next door to Chez Michel, its baby brother is equally popular and it's easy to see why. The blackboard menu offers similar but simpler dishes like celery root (celeriac) rémoulade with cured salmon, and pork belly on a bed of chard. The atmosphere is convivial and it's a great place to start or finish a trip to Paris, but service can be slow, so leave plenty of time if you have a train to catch or an appointment to make.
6 RUE DE BELZUNCE, 01 48 78 28 80

Chez Ginette de la Côte d'Azur

Behind the Sacré Coeur and off the beaten tourist track, this restaurant is hugely popular with locals, who congregate to enjoy the décor of curved and carved wood, the painted ceiling, and the vaguely Provençal-inspired menu of tuna carpaccio with arugula (rocket), grilled lamb with ratatouille, and cherry clafoutis. There's a small corner terrace for outdoor eating and a café for those who prefer to come here just for a coffee and so avoid the surprisingly high food prices.
101 RUE CAULINCOURT, 01 46 06 01 49

Lapin Braisé à la Bière

Rabbit braised in mustard and beer

A brasserie classic in the true sense of the word, this simple dish combines two favorites, rabbit and beer, to make a rich, warming stew. If you don't like rabbit, use chicken thighs instead.

SERVES 4
PREPARATION TIME: 10 MINUTES
COOKING TIME: ABOUT 2 HOURS

25g/1oz/2 tbsp butter	1 tbsp wholegrain mustard
1 tbsp olive oil	1 tbsp all-purpose (plain) flour
4 onions, peeled and	1 tbsp granulated sugar
thinly sliced	1 large sprig of fresh rosemary
salt and freshly ground	275ml/10fl oz/1¼ cups
black pepper	light beer
1 young rabbit, jointed, or	
8 chicken thighs	

Preheat the oven to 170°C/325°F/gas mark 3. Heat the butter and oil in a deep skillet (sauté pan) and fry the onions for 5–10 minutes over a low heat until pale golden.

Season the rabbit pieces (or chicken thighs) with salt and pepper and brush about half the mustard over one side of the meat. Put the meat mustard-side down in the skillet and fry for about 10 minutes, turning the pieces over until golden brown on both sides. Use a slotted spoon to transfer the contents of the pan to a heavy casserole with a lid.

Sprinkle the flour into the skillet, set it over a medium heat and stir. Add the sugar, rosemary, the rest of the mustard and the beer, stirring as you go.

Bring to a boil, season with salt and pepper, according to taste, and pour into the casserole dish. Cover and cook in the oven for about 1½ hours, until the rabbit is very tender and the sauce is slightly thickened. Serve immediately with the sauce poured over the rabbit.

Rémoulade de Céleri-rave au Saumon Mariné

Celery root (celeriac) rémoulade with cured salmon

Mustardy celery root rémoulade makes an excellent first course, but at Chez Casimir (page 23), they add grated carrot and partner it with home-cured salmon for a wonderful combination of colors and flavors. Cornichons and capers give the dish a sharper flavor.

SERVES 4–6
PREPARATION TIME: 20 MINUTES
COOKING TIME: 10 MINUTES

juice of 1 lemon	salt and freshly ground
1 celery root (celeriac)	white pepper
1 tbsp white wine vinegar	1 tbsp chopped capers
2 carrots, peeled	4–6 cornichons, very finely
3 large eggs	chopped
1 tbsp Dijon mustard	4–6 slices of cured or
250ml/9fl oz/1 cup olive oil	smoked salmon or gravlax

Pour the lemon juice into a large saucepan of water and bring to a boil. Peel the celery root and either cut into very fine julienne or coarsely grate it. Immediately drop the celeriac into the boiling water for 15–30 seconds, then drain thoroughly, place in a salad bowl and stir in half the vinegar. Cut into very fine julienne (or coarsely grate them) and add to the celery root.

Put two of the eggs in a small saucepan, and cover with cold water. Bring to a boil and cook the eggs for 8–10 minutes, then drain and run under cold water to stop them cooking. Peel and remove the whites.

Separate the remaining egg, reserving the yolk. Put the hard-boiled and raw egg yolks in a mortar with the mustard, and pound to a creamy paste. Whisk in the olive oil, a drop at a time, as if you were making mayonnaise. Once the sauce begins to thicken, you can start to trickle the oil in a little faster, stirring all the time. When the sauce has reached the consistency of mayonnaise, stir in the remaining vinegar and season with salt and pepper. Stir the sauce into the celery root and carrots, together with the chopped capers and cornichons, then chill.

Arrange the salmon on plates and pile the rémoulade on the side.

Restaurants

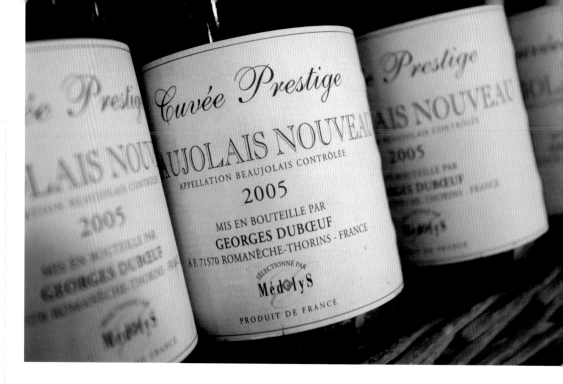

La Mère Catherine

A landmark on the place du Tertre, La Mère Catherine opened in 1793 and is reputed to be the oldest bistro in Paris. It was popular with occupying Russian troops in 1814 and the word "bistro" is said to derive from impatient Cossack soldiers shouting *"bistro!"* ("hurry up" in Russian) when overcome by hunger. The cheery, unpretentious restaurant, decked with red gingham tablecloths, still serves traditional bistro fare, with *soupe à l'oignon*, snails, and its specialty, *poulet cocotte*. For a typical French experience, finish with *îles flottantes* (floating meringue islands) or rich chocolate mousse. Wine from the Montmartre vineyard is occasionally on offer. There are a few outside tables and live music in the evenings.

6 PLACE DU TERTRE, 01 46 06 32 69

Chez Grisette

By day a restaurant, by night a wine bar, Grisette's cozy little establishment, perched in a steep, winding street, attracts a loyal and enthusiastic following. The short but always excellent menu changes twice weekly and is carefully chosen to partner the wines that Grisette travels all over France to find. Terrines are coarse and robustly flavored, the charcuterie and cheeses are excellent, and the blackboard menus are always tempting. The room is small, so be sure to reserve.

14 RUE HOUDON, 01 42 62 04 80

Julien

The seedy location belies the elegance of this archetypal belle-époque brasserie with its stained-glass skylights, art nouveau mirrors and polished mahogany bar. Classic dishes like salmon rillettes, foie gras, and fresh fish with buttery fennel are usually on offer. The *prix fixe* (fixed price) menu includes half a bottle of decent wine. It's worth ordering coffee for the home-made truffles that accompany it.

16 RUE DU FAUBOURG ST-DENIS, 01 47 70 12 06

Moulin de la Galette

One of Montmartre's only two remaining windmills houses a chic, touristy Italian restaurant offering standard fare. Inside the interior is light and roomy; however, it's worth a visit to sit outside on the charming terrace overlooking the jumble of back streets and courtyards. There's a good value Sunday brunch with scrambled eggs and croissants.

83 RUE LEPIC, 01 46 06 84 77

Le Palais des Rajpouts

Some of the cheapest and best Indian food in Paris can be found in the crumbling passage Brady. The vegetarian dishes are particularly enticing, from potato bhajis, and vegetable curries with creamy nut sauces to heavenly cardamom ice cream.

66 PASSAGE BRADY, 01 46 23 39 35
Other recommended restaurants in the passage include **Yasmin** (NOS. 71–73, 01 45 23 04 25), **La Reine du Kashmir** (NO. 80, 01 45 23 39 35), and **Pooja** (NO. 91, 01 48 24 00 83).

Au Pied du Sacré Coeur

Located right at the foot of the steps leading up to the Sacré Coeur, this small, very welcoming restaurant offers brasserie classics, like rabbit terrine with raisins and Cognac, and the spécialité de la maison, chicken breast with foie gras and figs. The chocolate délice lives up to its name and the cellar offers some excellent wines. On fine days, you can sit on the restaurant's terrace and gaze up at the church towering above you. Considering the location, prices are reasonable.

85 RUE LAMARCK, 01 46 06 15 26

Le Rajpout

From the gracious Indian doorman in colorful Rajasthani finery to the elegant interior with superb lamps and gilded tableware, eating here transports you to northern India. Choose from a fantastic array of dishes on the buffet. Curries are delicately spiced, the fish tikka is a treat, and the naan bread is freshly cooked. It's a world away from the insalubrious street outside.

12 RUE DU FAUBOURG ST-DENIS, 01 40 22 07 57

Terminus Nord

This huge belle-époque brasserie, now part of the Flo chain, is a welcome sight for hungry travelers emerging from Eurostar. Authentic brasserie dishes like soupe à l'oignon gratinée, grilled gigot of lamb, oysters, and other fruits de mer are always reliable. The tarte Tatin is excellent and the set menus and wines offer value for money.

23 RUE DE DUNKERQUE, 01 42 85 05 15

Chez Michel

As you might guess from the menu, chef-patron Thierry Breton comes from Brittany and his menu reflects his pride in the gourmet delights of his native land, so it's surprising that one wall of his simply decorated bistro is covered with a painting of Honfleur in Normandy. But the food is resolutely Breton. Fish and seafood are fresh and cooked with a light touch, there's a modern take on the typical Celtic stew *kig-ha farz*, and seasonal game is a highlight. Crisp *craquelins de St-Malo* (tartlets) are filled with aromatic goats' cheese, and the white chocolate and mint marquise, and hazelnut Paris-Brest are divine. Its proximity to the Gare du Nord makes it hugely popular, so advance booking is essential.

10 RUE DE BELZUNCE, 01 44 53 06 20

Montmartre Vineyard

Ever since the Romans built a temple to Bacchus on the hills of Montmartre, there have been vineyards on the butte. All that remains of the thriving industry is the Montmartre vineyard — a hidden treasure in the heart of the city, the vineyard is the last of its kind in Paris. It may be small, but it's possibly the prettiest and best maintained vineyard you'll ever see. The estate produces an impressive 500 bottles of red wine each year and is justifiably the pride of the neighborhood. The pressing of the grapes, which traditionally took place in the place du Tertre, now happens in specially designated *caves* (cellars) belonging to the 18th arrondissement's town hall.

In their heyday, three-quarters of the slopes in Montmartre were covered in grapevines, producing red and white wines, collectively known as le Picolo de Montmartre, which gave rise to the slang word *picoler* (to "hit the bottle"). The hedonistic nuns of the eighteenth-century Abbaye de Montmartre went in for a bit of picolage, but prudently set aside 1000 liters of wine to present to the monarch each year on the anniversary of his coronation. How much the king appreciated the gift is questionable; the acidic wine was incredibly diuretic that it was said every pint drunk produced a quarte of urine!

Sadly, by the beginning of the twentieth century, not a single vineyard remained in Montmartre. It wasn't until the 1930s that the mayor and other local worthies came up with the idea of planting vines on a small public square on the corner of the rue des Saules and rue St-Vincent (a highly appropriate location, as St-Vincent is the patron saint of wine). The Clos Montmartre is still here, perched high on a north-facing slope above the cemetery. The immaculately tended rows of mostly Gamay and Pinot Noir vines are interspersed with peach trees and splashy bright flowers, and in the fall, an arbor glows with a glorious fiery canopy of Virginia creeper. There's a spectacular view over the Montmartre cemetery and the rather more lively and appropriately bucolic *Au Lapin Agile* ("The Nimble Rabbit") cabaret club.

In all honesty, the wines the vineyard produces are more symbolic than drinkable, but every year about a 1000 bottles are produced and auctioned for charity at hugely inflated prices. For those who actually want to drink Clos de Montmartre, a few bottles are also sold at the *Syndicat d'Initiative* (tourist office) in the place du Tertre. However, if you are fortunate enough to be in the area in October, the annual three-day *Fête des Vendanges de Montmartre* to celebrate the grape harvest on the first Saturday has all the elements of a good street party. There's a Harvest Queen, fireworks, bands, and processions in which the local *confrérie du vin* (brotherhood of wine) is joined by others from various French wine-growing regions, bedecked in traditional robes and hung about with flags and oenological paraphernalia.

The vineyard is open to the public during the festival. The rest of the year it's unfortunately kept locked, but the wide bars of the iron entrance gate allow a good view of this curious remnant of Paris's once-thriving wine industry.

Moules Marinière

Seafood stands in Parisian markets display piles of gleaming black-shelled mussels labelled bouchots, which indicates that the molluscs are rope-grown and therefore virtually free of sand and grit, which makes them very easy to clean. Simply steamed with white wine and served with plenty of crusty fresh bread to mop up the juices, moules marinières make the perfect express supper.

SERVES 4
PREPARATION TIME: 15 MINUTES
COOKING TIME: 20 MINUTES

2.25kg/5lb mussels, preferably rope-grown
25g/1oz butter
2 shallots, peeled and finely chopped
2 garlic cloves, peeled and finely chopped
310ml/11fl oz dry white wine
1 bay leaf
sprig of thyme
2 tbsp chopped parsley
freshly ground black pepper

Wash the mussels in plenty of cold water, scrubbing the shells well. Give those that are open or gaping a sharp tap, and discard any mussels that do not close. Pull out the fibrous "beard" that sprouts between the shells.

Gently heat the butter in a large saucepan, add the shallots and garlic, and sweat until soft and translucent. Do not let them brown. Add the wine, bay leaf and thyme, and bring to the boil. Toss in the cleaned mussels, cover the saucepan with a tight-fitting lid, and steam over a high heat for 2 minutes, occasionally shaking the saucepan vigorously. Take off the lid and give the mussels a good stir, then put the lid back on and steam the mussels for another 1–2 minutes until they have all opened. Discard any that remain closed.

Use a slotted spoon to lift the mussels into warmed bowls. Season the cooking juices to taste and stir in the parsley. Pour the juices over the mussels, season with freshly ground black pepper and serve piping hot.

Paris-Brest

Choux pastry ring filled with praline mousseline

This indulgent pastry was created in 1891 by a pâtissier who used to watch the annual bicycle race between Paris and Brest from the doorway of his shop in the Paris suburbs. He was inspired to make this dessert in the shape of a bicycle wheel.

SERVES 6–8
PREPARATION TIME: ABOUT 15 MINUTES
COOKING TIME: 1 HOUR

CHOUX RING:
110ml/4fl oz/½ cup milk
110g/4oz/½ cup unsalted butter, diced
large pinch of salt
1 tsp superfine (caster) sugar
125ml/4½fl oz/½ cup water
150g/5oz/1¼ cups all-purpose (plain) flour
4 large eggs, lightly beaten
eggwash (1 large egg beaten with 1 tbsp milk), to glaze
3 tbsp toasted flaked almonds, for decoration
confectioners' (icing) sugar, for dusting

PRALINE CREAM:
6 egg yolks
200g/7oz/1 cup superfine (caster) sugar
125g/4½oz/packed 1 cup all-purpose (plain) flour
480ml/17fl oz/2 cups milk
250g/9oz/scant 1¼ cups unsalted butter
150g/5oz praline paste

Preheat the oven to 200°C/400°F/gas mark 6. Line a baking sheet with baking parchment.

To make the choux ring, combine the milk, butter, salt, sugar, and water in a saucepan. Bring to a boil over a low heat and take the pan off the heat the moment the mixture boils. Add the flour all at once and beat the mixture with a wooden spoon until it leaves the sides of the pan and looks smooth and shiny.

Return the saucepan to a medium heat for 1 minute, stirring continuously, to dry out the paste. Remove from the heat and let it cool for a few minutes, then beat in the eggs one at a time until completely amalgamated. Put the paste into a pastry bag with a 2-cm/¾-inch tip and pipe a 20–23-cm/8–9-inch ring on to the prepared baking sheet.

Brush lightly with the eggwash and sprinkle with the flaked almonds. Bake in the oven for about 30 minutes, until puffy and golden brown. Remove from the oven and transfer the ring on to a wire rack to cool.

Meanwhile, make the praline cream. Put the egg yolks, sugar, and flour into an electric mixer and whisk until pale and creamy. In a saucepan, bring the milk to a boil and strain it on to the egg mixture, whisking as you go to make a smooth cream. Pour this cream back into the saucepan and bring to a boil, whisking the mixture continuously.

Cook for 2 minutes, still whisking, then pour the cream back into the bowl of the mixer. Beat in half the butter and leave to cool. When the cream is cold, beat in the rest of the butter, then the praline paste.

Slice the choux ring in half horizontally, and place the bottom half on a serving plate. Put the praline cream in a pastry bag with a large star tip and pipe the cream into the bottom half of the choux ring. Put the other half of the choux ring on top, sprinkle over the almonds and dust with confectioners' sugar.

Landmarks

From the fascinating Cimetière de Montmartre, you can work up an appetite by climbing to the hilltop village of Montmartre. Its cobbled streets, whitewashed cottages, and steep stairways lined with iron lamps have an intimate atmosphere and it has retained much of its nineteenth-century charm. Here, you can stop at a pavement café for refreshment before visiting the tourist honeypots of place du Tertre and Basilique du Sacré Coeur, which dominates the butte. At sunset, the basilica's terrace affords unforgettable views of the city stretched out at its feet, and every evening, at the foot of the hill, the lighting of the Moulin Rouge's red sails shamelessly announces the start of the nightly revels.

Basilique du Sacré Coeur

As Eurostar draws close to the Gare du Nord, the shining white Basilica of the Sacred Heart (right) appears on the skyline. It's a dazzling sight; on a clear day, the brilliant white edifice with its cluster of domes and turrets looks more like a fairytale castle than a church. Dominating the butte, its unmistakable silhouette features the dazzling dome, the second highest point in Paris, inside which hangs one of the world's heaviest bells. It is well worth climbing the 234 steps to the top of the dome for the unforgettable panoramic view across the city, but it is definitely hard going, so take a cold drink and leave plenty of time. Inevitably, thousands of visitors throng the front steps, but many fewer bother to enter the basilica, the serene interior of which can still offer some spiritual refreshment.

Cimetière de Montmartre

Although it's not as famous as Père Lachaise, numerous composers and artists are buried in Montmartre's cemetery (below left). Alongside composers Berlioz and Offenbach lie the renowned writer Stendhal, and artists like Gustave Moreau and Edgar Degas. It was Degas who immortalized dancers in his paintings. It seems appropriate that Nijinsky's grave is here, along with the resting place of a very different kind of dancer, *La Goulue*, whose embonpoint and bawdy performances at the Moulin Rouge inspired the paintings of Toulouse-Lautrec. A map of the cemetery is available at the entrance.

Le Moulin Rouge

The red sails of the "windmill" (it was never actually a working mill) still entice you into the Moulin Rouge (top left), once a saucy

dance hall, immortalized by Toulouse-Lautrec. When it opened in 1889, the stage shows featuring scantily clad chorus girls dancing the can-can were considered scandalous. The most famous of the dancers who performed here were the willowy, elegant Jane Avril and the shameless Louise Weber, whose habit of draining the customers' drinks earned her the name *la Goulue* ("the glutton"). The shows still go on, but nowadays the exorbitant price of the cabaret and dinner is probably more shocking than the antics of the bare-breasted dancers bedecked in feathers and sequins, who still perform the can-can every night.

Place du Tertre

Bustling crowds of snap-happy tourists mingle with aspiring artists and street musicians in the animated tree-shaded square, which is Paris's highest point (*tertre* means hillock). Watch your pockets as you avoid or succumb to the lure of the caricaturists clamoring to sketch you, and persuasive painters flogging local landscapes. In winter, however, the delightful square retains its eighteenth-century charm. Avoid the expensive café in the middle and the mediocre, overpriced restaurants around the square; better to wander into the picturesque back streets for sustenance.

Champs-Elysées & Trocadéro

(8th, 16th & 17th arrondissements)

Watching the busy daytime crowds milling along the avenue des Champs-Elysées, dodging the traffic as they try to cross the wide avenue, it's hard to believe that just 500 years ago there was nothing here but open fields. In 1616, Marie de Medici created a long tree-lined driveway for the gentry to drive along in their carriages to see and be seen. When later that century the landscape gardener Le Nôtre transformed the driveway into beautiful parkland as a triumphal way out from the Tuileries, it inspired the name Champs-Elysées or "Elysian Fields".

Champs-Elysées & Trocadéro
(8th, 16th & 17th arrondissements)

By the mid-nineteenth century, le tout Paris was flocking to the Champs-Elysées, "the most beautiful avenue in the world", to admire the promenade of crinolined ladies and their dandy beaux, and the impressive military parades and royal processions that became a regular feature. Elegant restaurants and cafés were established among the trees and flowers, attracting a smart clientele.

Sadly, the avenue (below) has lost its heavenly aura. Elegant mansions still stand among gardens and trees at the place de la Concorde end, but the Champs becomes progressively less chic as you head up toward the Arc de Triomphe. It is still the gathering place for any French celebration — Bastille Day, New Year's Eve, the Tour de France — but the allure has faded. The once-elegant

boutiques sell tourist junk, the fashionable glaciers now sell bought-in ice creams, and the cafés have given way to burger bars and fast food joints. If hunger pangs strike as you stroll the mile from one end of the Champs-Elysées to the other (a good half-hour walk), you would be well advised to give these a wide berth and divert into the side streets to find, decent affordable food.

It's not all doom and gloom, however. Thanks to an initiative by President Jacques Chirac, possibly intended as a boost to Paris's dashed hopes of hosting the 2012 Olympic Games, the Champs-Elysées has recently had a facelift and something of its former glory is re-emerging. The Grand and Petit Palais have been restored, and the elegant streets behind the Arc de Triomphe are full of chic restaurants. Not all the updates have met with universal approval. The landmark Publicis Drugstore, a favorite haunt of tourists in search of a late-night club sandwich or snack, and a model of 1950s architecture, has had a makeover. The formerly staid facade has been hyper-modernized into a glass extravaganza more in keeping with Las Vegas than Haussmann's Paris, and the snack menu now consists of expensive designer nibbles aimed at willowy women who shop in the couture boutiques in nearby avenue Montaigne. But the twinkling fiber-optic lights outside the entrance merely reflect the general tackiness of the as yet unreconstructed food outlets on the other side of the street.

The western end of the Champs-Elysées is dominated by the Arc de Triomphe, the monument Napoleon planned to celebrate his own glory and military might. It stands on the officially renamed place Charles de Gaulle, still known to all as "l'Etoile", from the twelve avenues that radiate from it like beams from a star. It's traffic bedlam, with cars converging from all directions and no apparent right of way, especially not for pedestrians. Unless you have a death wish, use the subway to access the center, and climb the 282 narrow steps or take the elevator to the top of the Arc de Triomphe and forget the nightmare below as you gaze at the breathtaking view over the

web of Haussmann's avenues. Look south to see the awesome vista of the terraces of the place du Trocadéro and the gleaming bronze statues of the Palais de Chaillot, with the Eiffel Tower looming behind. The area is always bustling and is enlivened by the twice-weekly Marché Président Wilson close by, where you can buy some of the finest and freshest produce in Paris, sit by a fountain in the Jardins du Trocadéro, and enjoy a picnic of bread, delicious cheese, and fresh fruit. If you prefer to sit indoors, there are plenty of cafés nearby where you can get light snacks and lunches.

Spreading to the west and south of the Arc de Triomphe are the impossibly elegant streets and gorgeous mansions of the 16th and 17th arrondissements, home to diplomats, wealthy executives, and celebrities, who can afford to patronize the wealth of haute couture shops, haute cuisine restaurants, and high end food shops. Dinner in one of the Michelin-starred establishments here will cost a fortune, but the experience will be unforgettable. If your budget won't stretch that far, you'll find an amazing range of gourmet foods on offer in the chic rue de Lévis and rue de l'Annonciation. Buy a selection of breads, cheese, pastries, and fruit and create your own haute cuisine repast.

Pages 34–5: one of the superbly decorated eighteenth-century lamps that adorn the columns on the Jardin des Tuileries side of the place de la Concorde.

Alléosse

Parisians will cross Paris for Alléosse's renowned seasonal époisses de Bourgogne cheese and perfectly aged St-Marcellin, along with a host of other exceptional cows' and goats' milk cheeses, some rare and all brought to the peak of maturity. It's best to go during the week, as the shop is always crowded with shoppers on Saturdays.

13 RUE PONCELET, 01 46 22 50 45

Les Caves Augé

Said to be the oldest wine shop in Paris, and much frequented by Marcel Proust, les Caves Augé opened in 1850 and still retains its original charm. There's a vast range of fine wines personally selected by the owner, Marc Silbard. Friendly, knowledgeable experts guide you through the selection of rare vintages, including some fabulous bottles of Bordeaux.

116 BOULEVARD HAUSSMANN,
01 45 22 16 97

Marché Président Wilson

The stretch between Trocadéro and place d'Iéna comes alive on Wednesday and Saturday mornings from 7am, with the arrival of one of Paris's best roving markets. Interspersed with clothes, leather goods, jewelry, and flowers are stalls selling every sort of food imaginable to tempt your tastebuds. Perfectly ripened fruit and the freshest vegetables vie with the abundant flowers for color and artistic arrangement; Joël Thiébaut's fresh herbs come in all the colors of the rainbow; cheeses are in prime condition; artisan breads, cakes, and Viennoiserie are freshly baked. The market caters to the cream of Parisian society, so everything here is of the highest quality, from the spanking-fresh seafood on Jacky Lorenzo's stall, to the spit-roasted free-range chickens and ducks, and Patrick Leconte's superb charcuterie. If you're in the mood for exotic food, look for Reininger's North African spice stall, or the Lebanese and Italian traiteurs. There's a small organic section at the place d'Iéna end. Go as early as possible to get the best selection of produce, because this popular market becomes incredibly crowded as the morning progresses.

AVENUE DU PRESIDENT WILSON

Les Caves Taillevent

Closely linked with the venerable Taillevent restaurant, these two vast cellars contain almost half a million bottles of the finest wines, some of them extremely rare. There's nothing condescending about the expert advice on hand; whether you're a wine buff or a novice, you'll be made to feel welcome.

199 RUE DU FAUBOURG ST-HONORÉ,
01 45 61 14 09

La Ferme de Passy Fromagerie

This little cheese shop stocks a fantastic range of regional and seasonal cheeses, all matured to smelly perfection. If you love époisses and Comté, this is the place for you. There's a large selection of artisan goats' cheeses, and "foreign curiosities" like Stilton with port.
39 RUE DE L'ANNONCIATION,
01 42 88 14 93

Fouquet

Fouquet has been making exquisite chocolates by hand since 1852. It's hard to choose between liqueur-filled creations, nuts and marzipan enrobed in fondant, or the specialty *salvators* (bite into the hard chocolate coating, which shatters to reveal the soft caramel within) — they are all divine. If chocolate's not your thing, there are jams, jellies, marzipan fruits rolled in sugar crystals, and delectable macaroons.
22 RUE FRANÇOIS PREMIER,
01 47 23 30 36

Geneviève Lethu

You'll find a treasure trove of largely Provençal-inspired housewares in this branch of Geneviève Lethu's kitchenware stores. It's a great place for buying presents for gourmet friends — from fantasy wine-stoppers and sparklers for celebration cakes to attractive and unusual tableware, linens, kitchen equipment, and gadgets.
1 AVENUE NIEL, 01 45 72 03 47

La Maison du Chocolat

Everything is chocolate- and cream-colored in this treasure house, where the legendary Robert Linxe has been making the most sophisticated and delectable chocolates for almost thirty years, and every one is a chocoholic's delight. Unusual flavorings appear in his truffles — juniper and rosemary, bergamot and raspberry. Impossible to choose. Even the boxes are works of art.
89 AVENUE RAYMOND POINCARÉ,
01 40 67 77 83

Pascal le Glacier

There's nothing much to see when you enter Pascal Combette's shop, but ranged inside the freezer cabinets are some of the best sorbets and ice creams in Paris, rivalling even the famous Berthillon. Flavors change with the seasons, but there's always a choice of about thirty ice creams and the same selection of sorbets, sold by the liter or in individual pots. How do you choose between mocha ice cream with coffee beans, chocolate and marrons glacés, *pavé de Passy* (chocolate and chestnut slice), honey nougat, salted caramel, or Provençal fig, lichee, and saké, or *fraise des bois* (strawberry) sorbets? From April through October, there are takeout ice cream cones.
17 RUE BOIS LE VENT, 01 45 27 61 84

Pavillon Elysée Lenôtre

Lenôtre's elegant historical mansion at the Concorde end of the Champs-Elysées is a temple to gastronomy and a gourmet's paradise. The boutique sells Lenôtre's incomparable pâtisserie and cakes, along with the finest teas, coffees, and chocolates. If you aspire to create these delicacies yourself, discover the secrets at the Lenôtre Ecole de

Cuisine, then visit the shop to buy the necessary professional utensils, innovative accessories, and cookery books to inspire you. If this all seems too daunting, indulge yourself in the beautiful terrace restaurant.
10 AVENUE DES CHAMPS-ELYSÉES,
01 42 65 85 10

Tarte Julie

The sweet and savory tarts displayed in the window of this branch of the Tarte Julie chain could easily be passed off as home-made. Who wouldn't be proud of preparing a tart with a generous filling of duck confit, onion, and potato, or goats' cheese and spinach? Delectable chocolate tarts are combined with banana or pear, and the purple-and-gold celebration tart mixes a medley of different plums with apricots. Buy a whole tart or just a slice to eat in the cozy shop or to takeout.
14 RUE DE L'ANNONCIATION,
01 45 20 60 14

Restaurants in Champs-Elysées & Trocadéro

Taillevent

Named after Guillaume Tirel, the fourteenth-century chef known as Taillevent, this is Paris's most enduring "grand" restaurant. Despite the refined elegance of the paneled rooms (the back room is more casual), elegance and simplicity abound. This ensures that dining here is a relaxed experience, and although most diners dress up for the occasion, ties are not de rigueur for men.

The innovative head chef, Alain Solivérès, brings a light modern touch to the cooking, with dishes such as unctuous foie gras, crème brûlée with tonka beans (black, aromatic beans from South America), earthy spelt risotto with frogs' legs, and John Dory with a heavenly saffron jus redolent of the south. Bitter chocolate and tea gourmandise or macaronade round a meal off perfectly. For food and surroundings of this quality, prices are not outrageous. However, the biggest bargain is the set lunchtime menu. This changes regularly and features Alain Solivérès's latest seasonal creations.

15 RUE LAMENNAIS, 01 44 95 15 01

Le Bois le Vent

It's refreshing to find a good value Lebanese restaurant in such an upmarket area. Local residents flock to enjoy the exceptional mezze with evocative names: baba ganouche, fattouche, and *mdararda* (lentils with onions and rice). Special variations on tartares include raw lamb fillet. For the less adventurous, there's a terrific selection of vegetarian dishes and grilled meats. Finish with nut-filled baklava or *mouhlabieh*, a Lebanese variation on crème caramel.

59 RUE DE BOULAINVILLIERS, 01 40 50 75 73

Chez André

Unchanged since it opened in 1937, this art nouveau brasserie is something of a Paris institution. Well-heeled businessmen and locals tuck into plentiful platters of the freshest seafood, along with classics like sole meunière, roast rack of lamb, and grilled veal kidneys, and a changing plat du jour (bouillabaisse on Fridays). Desserts include old favorites like gorgeously fattening rum babas and millefeuilles oozing a delicious pastry cream.

12 RUE MARBOEUF, 01 47 20 59 57

Le Fouquet's

Once just a smart venue at which to see and be seen, Fouquet's new chef has made this Paris institution a great — if expensive — place to eat as well. Classic French dishes are given a lighter, more refined treatment: turbot is cooked with squid sauce and zucchini (courgette) flowers, scallops with mango and leeks. You will still find traditional dishes like grilled lamb, and delicious desserts. The old-fashioned red plush décor remains unchanged,

making Fouquet's a comfortable yet glamorous place to eat. If you enjoy people-watching, join the French show-biz celebrities at a table on the veranda.
99 AVENUE DES CHAMPS-ELYSÉES, 01 47 23 70 60

Guy Savoy

Prices are stratospheric but so is the quality of Guy Savoy's hugely inventive cooking. It's a delight to be warmly welcomed into the unstuffy, calm, pale-wood dining rooms and relax with an amuse-bouche — perhaps a minuscule foie gras club sandwich — before the gastronomic theater begins. The wine list is so huge that it comes on its own trolley. Another trolley is laden with a dozen breads, a different flavor to accompany each course. Dégustation menus allow you to sample the best of Guy Savoy's dazzling cooking:

langoustines, John Dory with unctuous pumpkin and white truffle sauce, then there's a signature dish of artichoke soup with black truffle. Move on through a series of seasonal dishes: poached and roasted wild duck with confit chestnuts, or roasted foie gras with cabbage. Each glorious dish is presented with artistry and wit. Impossible to resist the extraordinary array of delicious cheeses, and the scrumptious chocolate fondant layered with praline, and a Belgian endive (chicory) sauce that is to die for. Take out a mortgage and go once for an unforgettable gastronomic experience.
18 RUE TROYEN, 01 43 80 40 61

Le Kiosque

The brainchild of a journalist, this convivial restaurant takes the theme of newspapers. The idea is carried through from the daily papers hanging on wooden poles to the delivery boy's bicycle suspended from the ceiling and the newspaper-wrapped menu. The set menu might include swordfish carpaccio with citrus, caramelized duck magret with balsamic reduction, and must-have desserts include a melting chocolate fondant and unusual ice creams. The *menu copine* (menu for two) is made for sharing — two main courses and a glass of Champagne each.
1 PLACE DE MEXICO, 01 47 27 96 98

Pages 42–3: the fifteenth-century floodlit fountains at the place de la Concorde.

Rouget Barbet Poêlé, Brandade de Merlu et Aïoli

Red mullet with brandade of hake and aïoli

I ate this wonderful dish, bursting with Provençal flavors and colors, at Taillevent, one of Paris's most elegant and sophisticated restaurants, and asked chef Alain Solivérès to give me the recipe. As most of us, sadly, don't have the skill or kitchen back-up of a three-star chef, I have adapted his recipe to make it more accessible to cooks at home.

SERVES 4

PREPARATION TIME: 45 MINUTES

COOKING TIME: ABOUT 1½ HOURS

4 red mullet, filleted

50ml/2fl oz/¼ cup olive oil

4 baby scallions
 (spring onions)

4tsp ready-made tapenade

4 pieces of tomato confit or
 marinated roasted tomatoes

50ml/2fl oz/¼ cup basil oil

BRANDADE:

200ml/7fl oz/⅞ cup milk

1 sprig of fresh thyme

1 bay leaf

1 garlic clove, peeled
 and halved

50g/2oz fingerling (salad)
 potatoes

110g/4oz hake fillet

1tbsp olive oil

10 garlic cloves, peeled and
 chopped

200ml/7fl oz/⅞ cup heavy
 whipping cream

salt and freshly ground black
 pepper

AIOLI:

2 baking potatoes

handful of coarse cooking salt

2 garlic cloves, peeled and
 finely chopped

2 large egg yolks

pinch of powdered saffron

400ml/14fl oz/1¾ cups olive oil

4tsp fish stock

Preheat the oven to 240°C/475°F/gas mark 9. Put the baking potatoes for the aïoli on a baking sheet on a bed of coarse salt and bake for about 1 hour until soft.

Meanwhile, make the brandade. Bring the milk with the thyme, bay leaf, and garlic to a boil, turn off the heat and leave to infuse. Boil the fingerling potatoes in salted water until almost tender. Remove the thyme, bay leaf, and garlic from the milk and add them to the potato water. Cook the potatoes for another 2–4 minutes, until the tip of a sharp knife can be easily inserted. Drain the potatoes, reserving the water, then peel and crush the potatoes. Stir in 2 tablespoons of the infused water as you crush the potatoes.

Put the hake in a saucepan, pour on the potato infused milk and poach the fish for about 4 minutes until the flesh just flakes. Drain, reserving the milk.

Heat the olive oil in a skillet (frying pan) over a low heat, add the chopped garlic, and sweat it for 2–3 minutes until soft. Add the hake and cook until all the moisture has evaporated, then add the crushed potatoes. Stir vigorously until smooth, loosen with a little of the reserved milk, then stir in the cream and season to taste.

When the potatoes for the aïoli are cooked, halve them and scoop out the flesh. Mix in the garlic and put the potatoes in an electric mixer. At medium speed, add the egg yolks one by one, and then add the saffron. Increase the speed and gradually add the oil in a thin, steady stream, as for mayonnaise, until the aïoli is very smooth. Stir in the fish stock, and refrigerate.

Season the red mullet fillets and sauté them, along with the scallions, in olive oil for about 2 minutes on each side until golden.

Lay each fish fillet on the side of a warmed plate and garnish with the tapenade, tomato confit, and scallions. Divide the brandade between the four plates, heaping it in the middle. Put a spoonful of aïoli beside the fish. Drizzle basil oil over everything.

Canard Rôti au Miel et aux Epices

Roast duck with honey and spices

The Romans used honey and spices to complement the richness of duck and the combination has stood the test of time, as you will see when you taste this glorious dish. Black cherry jam makes a fabulous substitute for the honey.

SERVES 4
PREPARATION TIME: 10 MINUTES
COOKING TIME: 10–15 MINUTES

4 duck magrets (boneless breasts) or legs
freshly ground black pepper
8 cloves
4 tbsp runny honey
juice of ½ lemon

½ tsp ground mixed spices (ginger and cinnamon)
2 whole star anise
150ml/5fl oz/⅔ cup chicken stock

Score the duck skin in a criss-cross pattern without cutting into the flesh. Season lightly with pepper. Stick 2 cloves into either end of each magret or leg. Mix the honey and lemon juice with the ground spices and star anise, and brush the mixture all over the duck.

Heat a large non-stick skillet (frying pan) until very hot, put in the duck pieces skin-side down along with the remaining lemon and honey mixture, and cook for 3–4 minutes, until the fat begins to run and the skin becomes sticky and brown. Turn the duck pieces over and cook on the other side for another 3–4 minutes for magrets or 4 minutes for legs.

Take the duck out of the pan, remove the cloves, pour off the excess fat and keep the duck warm.

Pour in the stock and boil until reduced by half, scraping up the caramelized juices from the bottom of the pan.

Put the duck on warmed plates, pour a little sauce around it, and serve with a green salad.

Restaurants in Champs-Elysées & Trocadéro

Ladurée

The original grand salon de thé of this famous pâtissier is near the Madeleine church on rue Royale, but this ornate Second Empire offshoot with its wood paneling, gilded mirrors, and painted ceiling adds a touch of class to the Champs-Elysées. Here, forty-five pastry chefs and forty cooks prepare a wealth of traditional and festive treats. The pastries match up to the over-the-top setting: Ladurée's world famous melt-in-the-mouth macaroons come in twenty different flavors, the hot chocolate is divine, and customers jostle to buy the irresistible cakes, croissants, and pains au chocolat. If you fancy more than a dainty snack, the menu offers omelets, salads, and sandwiches, plus more substantial dishes at lunchtime and dinner.

75 AVENUE DES CHAMPS-ELYSÉES,
01 40 75 08 75

Ledoyen

The food is as opulent as the setting in this elegant eighteenth-century building in the Champs-Elysées gardens. Chef Christian Le Squer serves wonderfully creative dishes with wit and style — a single Brussels sprout accompanies a breast of pheasant stuffed with its own liver. Crunchy sautéed langoustines have a citrus-oil tang, and heavenly truffled crushed potatoes accompany braised turbot. Cheeses have been matured to perfection, and the deliciously crisp chocolate slivers sandwiched with mascarpone and served with aromatic coffee sorbet will send you heavenward. If you've won the lotto, feel free to indulge in a ceremonial shaving of white truffles in season with your chosen dish.

CARRÉ DES CHAMPS-ELYSÉES,
01 53 05 10 00

Le Musée du Vin

Paris's Museum of Wine is housed in the vaulted cellars of the fourteenth-century Abbey de Passy, just behind the rue des Eaux, where a vineyard once flourished above a spring. Winding passageways guide you through the rich and diverse history of wine in France, with a fascinating collection of old wine-making implements, wine glasses, and paraphernalia, and an enchanting terracotta statue of a baby Bacchus. Waxwork tableaux bring the vine-growing and wine-making processes to life and tastings are available. Admission to the museum is free if you eat in the restaurant (open at lunchtime only).

5–7 SQUARE CHARLES DICKENS,
01 45 25 63 26

Le Petit Rétro

Take a step back in time at this pretty, atmospheric 1900s bistro, whose two rooms (the front one is non-smoking) have art nouveau flower-painted tiled walls and a welcoming ambience. Seasonal dishes include earthy wild mushroom fricassée. Offal is a specialty and might come as a generous portion of foie gras melting over a pile of fresh tagliatelle. Boudin noir comes encased in crisp pastry with fried apples, and richly sauced snails are presented under a pastry hat. Leave room for profiteroles with an unctuous chocolate sauce, and enjoy an espresso made in the original 1900s machine.

5 RUE MESNIL, 01 44 05 06 05

1728

Dining at this most elegant eighteenth-century town house, once the residence of General Lafayette, is like walking into history. The Chinese owners have lovingly restored the glorious wood paneling and painted ceilings in the three rooms. Dine under a vast chandelier and huge eighteenth-century tapestry in the stupendous Salle Pompadour, with its pink marble tables, gold cornices, and opulent blue silk drapes, or choose the more discreet paneled Salle Lafayette, or the music room. The Euro-Japanese menu offers deliciously tender lamb and beef with honeyed, spicy Oriental flavors, marinated scallops enrobed in Chinese truffles and lightly sautéed, or a 1728 Turco-Mongolian version of steak tartare. The salted chocolate Mikado is a highlight of the exquisite desserts by Pierre Hermé.

8 RUE D'ANJOU, 01 40 17 04 77

L'Appart'

Eating here is like dining in someone's home. Each part of this cozy, welcoming restaurant is like a different comfortable room. Whether you opt for the cellar, kitchen, library with its inglenook fireplace, or the elegant dining room, you'll enjoy modern French dishes with the subtle addition of spices and exotic flavors. Start with one of the justly famous cocktails before embarking on delicious marinated salmon sashimi, or roast lamb with pumpkin purée, and perhaps a lemon tart topped with soft meringue to finish.

9 RUE DU COLISÉE, 01 53 75 42 00

Tarte au Saumon et aux Epinards

Salmon and spinach tart

Salmon and spinach are a winning combination, and an appetizing-looking tart in the window of Tarte Julie inspired me to create my own version. Instead of one large tart, you could make six elegant tartlets if you want to impress your guests.

SERVES 6

PREPARATION TIME: 15 MINUTES, PLUS CHILLING THE PASTRY

COOKING TIME: ABOUT 1 HOUR FOR A LARGE TART,

30 MINUTES FOR TARTLETS

350g/12oz pie dough (shortcrust pastry)

110g/4oz baby spinach leaves

350g/8oz salmon fillet, skinned and cut into 2.5-cm/1-inch cubes

large pinch of paprika or a grating of nutmeg

2 large eggs, plus 2 egg yolks

340ml/12fl oz/1½ cups heavy whipping cream

salt and freshly ground black pepper

2tbsp grated Gruyère cheese

Roll out the pastry on a floured surface and use it to line a 23-cm/9-inch loose-bottomed tart pan (flan tin). Prick the base all over and mark the edges with a fork. Refrigerate for 30 minutes.

Preheat the oven to 200°C/400°F/gas mark 6. Fill the pastry shell with baking parchment and pie weights (baking beans), and bake blind in the oven for 12–15 minutes. Remove the weights (beans) and paper and bake for another 5 minutes. Take the tart pan out of the oven and reduce the oven temperature to 180°C/350°F/gas mark 4.

Put a layer of some of the spinach in the pastry shell and arrange the salmon evenly on top. Dust with paprika or nutmeg, and then scatter the rest of the spinach over the salmon.

In a large bowl, beat the eggs, yolks, and cream together and season with salt and pepper. Pour over the salmon and spinach. Sprinkle the top with the cheese.

Bake for 30–40 minutes, until the filling is just set and the top is nicely browned. Remove from the oven and serve hot or warm.

Crêpes Suzettes

SERVES 4

PREPARATION TIME: 5 MINUTES, PLUS 30 MINUTES TO REST BATTER

COOKING TIME: 15 MINUTES

CREPE BATTER:

110g/4oz/1 cup all-purpose (plain) flour

pinch of salt

1 large egg, plus 1 egg yolk

275ml/10fl oz/1¼ cups milk

125g/4½oz/½ cup butter, melted, for cooking

ORANGE SAUCE:

2 oranges, washed and dried

8 sugar cubes

50g/2oz/⅓ cup superfine (caster) sugar

juice of 1 lemon (optional)

zest of 1 orange, very finely shredded

110g/4oz/½ cup unsalted butter, diced

2tbsp Cointreau (or Grand Marnier)

2tbsp Cognac

To make the batter, put all the ingredients except the melted butter in a bowl and whisk until smooth. Leave to rest for 30 minutes.

Brush a small skillet (crêpe pan) with melted butter and heat until it sizzles. Pour in just enough batter to cover the bottom in a very thin layer and tip the skillet to spread it evenly. Cook the crêpe for 30–60 seconds on one side, until golden underneath, then flip or toss it over and cook for 30–60 seconds on the other side. Lightly brush the pan with butter and continue to make twelve very thin crêpes, laying each one on paper towels as it is ready.

To make the sauce, hold the oranges over a large skillet and rub the sugar cubes all over the skins. When the cubes start to crumble, let them drop into the pan. Halve and squeeze the oranges and strain the juice. Set the skillet over a medium heat and sprinkle in the superfine sugar. When it starts to caramelize and turn golden, stir in the strained orange juice and simmer for a few moments.

Lay a crêpe in the sauce, then turn it to coat both sides. Fold it into quarters and place on a warmed serving plate. Treat all the crêpes in this way and arrange three on a plate.

If the remaining sauce looks sticky, thin it with a little lemon juice. Bring a pan of water to the boil and blanch the orange zest. Remove with a slotted spoon, add to the sauce and bring to a boil, then lower the heat and whisk in the butter, one piece at a time, until the sauce is shiny. Stir in the Cointreau and pour over the crêpes. Heat the Cognac in a very small saucepan. Pour it over the crêpes, and light it with a long taper, and serve with crème fraîche.

Chocolate

Parisians have an abiding love affair with chocolate. They consume it at any time of day, from a cup of fragrant, steaming hot chocolate at breakfast to a flaky pain au chocolat for morning coffee, then perhaps a macaroon with more hot chocolate at le 4 o'clock, and a dense, dark chocolate truffle after dinner. Of course, they take chocolate very seriously and only the best will do. The finest Parisian artisan chocolatiers are true masters of their craft and create the most refined, delicious, and artistic chocolates in the world. In Paris, chocolate is treated with the same respect as fine wine.

At the annual Salon du Chocolat in October, an orgy of chocolate consumption which attracts more than 120,000 visitors each year, lectures and discussions (or "chocologues") include such rarefied topics as "The Role of Soil in the Gustatory Expression of Terroir" and "A Geopolitical History of Chocolate". The event is a chocolate extravaganza like no other, with exhibits running the gamut from fabulous bouquets of flowers to life-size sculptures, and exquisite haute couture outfits complete with shoes and handbags, all entirely hand-crafted from chocolate.

Chocolate is not a French creation; it first arrived in Europe in the sixteenth century, when the Spanish conquistador and conqueror of Mexico, Hernandos Cortés, brought it back to Spain, extolling its aphrodisiac qualities. Naturally, the French court embraced this food of love with enthusiasm, and Louis XIII was delighted when his Austrian bride insisted on importing her own supplies of chocolate from Spain to Paris. At that time, chocolate was always drunk, not eaten in solid form; whisking up the perfect brew required the skill of a barman concocting a cocktail. It was only in 1659 that the king permitted the first chocolate shop to open in Paris. At Versailles, Marie Antoinette even employed her own personal chocolatier, who secreted almost half of France's cache of the precious "brown gold" in the royal storerooms, ensuring that it remained an almost exclusive preserve of the court.

The reputation of chocolate as an aphrodisiac gave rise to intense debate. Was it potentially dangerous and intoxicating or did it possess genuine health-giving qualities? The chocolatier Monsieur Debauve and his pharmacist friend Monsieur Gallet hit on the idea of promoting its beneficial effects. They opened a combined pharmacy and chocolate shop to sell "chocolate treatments" — medicinal blends of chocolate with almond milk to aid digestion, and orange blossom to calm the nerves (you can still buy these chocolates in the shop in the rue des Sts-Pères today). They even designed a special, intensely masculine blend for Napoleon, with faint, subtle undertones of tobacco and spice, to increase his potency in love and war.

Today's Parisian maître chocolatiers fashion chocolate into divine works of art, as ravishing to the eye as to the palate. They scour the world for the finest cocoa beans and flavorings, and use their personal alchemy to blend them into the world's most refined, aromatic, intoxicating chocolate. Sophisticated flavorings are used to intrigue the palate: fennel, cinnamon, ylang-ylang, citrus zest, and even cheese make unexpected appearances enrobed in deep, dark, bitter chocolate. Designer chocolates are gilded with pure gold leaf or molded into intricate flowers, shells, and animals, and packed into boxes worthy of the finest jewels. Window displays are spectacular, as befits this most delectable of foods, and are worthy of an haute couture boutique. The French for window-shopping is *lécher les vitrines* ("lick the windows") and it's hard to resist the temptation of doing just that as you feast your eyes on the glorious wares in the chocolate shops of Paris.

Landmarks

Brave the traffic to reach the place de la Concorde, the largest square in Paris, look westward, and you'll be rewarded with a fantastic view of the city's most famous thoroughfare, the Champs-Elysées, stretching up to the majestic Arc de Triomphe. The magnificent archway was commissioned by Napoleon Bonaparte, and was the site of a lavish and triumphant procession even before it was finished. It still remains the venue for national celebrations — the pomp and ceremony of Bastille Day and the last leg of the Tour de France in July and the Armistice celebrations in November. Today the area has 300,000 residents and a further 100,000 people come to work here each day.

Arc de Triomphe

Delusions of grandeur led Napoleon to commission the Arc de Triomphe (below left) in 1809 as a monument to his military triumphs, just at the moment his empire started to crumble. He never saw the world's largest arch completed; it was not finished until 1836, fifteen years after his death. But his dream of a monument to himself was fulfilled, as a list of his victories is carved around the arch, and there's a fine frieze of battle scenes around the base. To see the Arc and Champs-Elysées at their best, visit early in the morning, when the light brings out the details of the sculptures, or in the evening as the sun is setting. At night, the view of the shimmering lights of the city is utterly magical.

Grand and Petit Palais

Newly restored to gleaming glory, the magnificent turtle-shaped glass and iron roof of the Grand Palais with its belle-époque pinnacle can be seen for miles around. Together with the Petit Palais and the Eiffel Tower, it was built as a temporary structure for the *Exposition Universelle* of 1900, but no one has ever dared to demolish them. Since the Crystal Palace in London burnt down, the colossal 788-feet-long Grand Palais has remained the largest ironwork-and-glass structure in the world. The three facades were each designed by a different architect; it's worth wandering round the perimeter to admire the striking mix of neo-classical and art nouveau decoration, particularly the friezes on the eastern and western facades. The eastern side of the palace hosts popular art exhibitions, while the western side has a fascinating science museum, called the Palais de la Découverte.

Across the road is the Petit Palais, with its decorative mosaics and sculpted friezes. It houses the Musée des Beaux-Arts de la Ville, a collection of mainly nineteenth-century paintings by artists such as Manet and Renoir.

Palais de Chaillot

Built high above the Seine for the *Exposition Universelle* of 1937, the honey-colored Palais de Chaillot (above) offers fantastic views of the River Seine and the Eiffel Tower. It is a striking example of art deco architecture, adorned with sculptures, with its two symmetrical curved colonnaded wings embracing the terraces of the Trocadéro.

It houses the huge Musée de la Marine and what's left of the anthropological museum, although most of the exhibits, at the time of writing, are in storage, awaiting a move to a new museum. Although the inside may be of limited interest, the terraces are always lively, with street artists, souvenir sellers, and food kiosks offering snacks of dubious quality.

Place de la Concorde

The impressive place de la Concorde and its fountains were laid out to designs by the architect Gabriel in the 1750s as a setting for an equestrian statue of Louis XV and it was named after the monarch, but during the revolution the statue was removed and the guillotine took its place. Over 1000 royals and aristocrats were beheaded here, including Louis XVI and his arrogant queen Marie Antoinette, who paid the price for her infamous remark to the peasants who were starving for lack of bread: "*qu'ils mangent de la brioche*" ("let them eat cake"). The square was renamed place de la Concorde in 1795 in the hope of peaceful times ahead. It is one of the most elegant squares in Paris, with its ornate tiered fountains, ancient Egyptian obelisk, and the colonnaded mansions that surround it. The eight statues in the four corners of the square represent the cities of Lille, Strasbourg, Lyon, Marseille, Bordeaux, Nantes, Brest, and Rouen.

Faubourg St-Honoré, Madeleine & Opéra

(1st, 8th & 9th arrondissements)

No street name could be less appropriate for the grandest street in Paris than "Faubourg". Meaning "fake borough", it was the derogatory term applied to Paris's first suburbs — a far cry from the sheer elegance of today's main shopping avenue, the Faubourg St-Honoré. It passes between the imposing buildings of the President's Elysée Palace and the Ministry of the Interior, where it becomes the rue St-Honoré and continues past the incomparable place Vendôme and alongside the tranquil greenery of the Jardin des Tuileries in the 1st arrondissement.

Faubourg St-Honoré, Madeleine & Opéra
(1st, 8th & 9th arrondissements)

The area was designated number one arrondissement in 1860 because of its location at the heart of the city, but it is also one of the oldest, grandest, most beautiful, greenest, and least populated quarters in Paris. Only the mega-wealthy can afford to live in the historic apartments built above the dazzling jewelers and oh-so-desirable art and antiques dealers. And only the rich can aspire to stay in the luxury hotels that proliferate along and around the rue de Rivoli, and to dine at some of Paris's most exclusive restaurants.

Even if you can't afford to live in a sumptuous apartment here, it's a wonderful area in which to stroll and drink in the beauty of the many protected buildings. If you need to stop and rest your feet, sitting down in a café will cost you; better, perhaps, to perch on a slatted chair by a fountain in the Jardin des Tuileries and watch the children sailing little boats on the mini-lake. For a more urban retreat, walk eastward along the rue St-Honoré and go through the courtyard of a great glass office block to the almost entirely pedestrianized Marché St-Honoré, where cafés and snack bars offer an outdoor haven. It's a very pleasant place to sit and have a cup of coffee or a snack at affordable prices.

Not surprisingly, this whole area is a gourmet's delight. There may be a dearth of cheap and cheerful markets and bargain food shops, but in the streets around the Madeleine in the 8th arrondissement you will find the gourmet equivalent of haute couture boutiques and precious jewels. Here you can rub shoulders with the sophisticated inhabitants of the quarter and the thousands of tourists who come to worship at the shrine of gastronomy. There is the iconic Fauchon, whose exquisite window displays invite you to enter a paradise on earth for foodies, and its smaller scale but no less luxurious counterpart, Hédiard. Fauchon has a salon de thé and Hédiard a restaurant where — at a price — you can sample the delicacies on sale downstairs. And who could resist a slice of *gâteau St-Honoré*, a rich pastry ring filled with crème patissière or whipped cream and

crowned with a coronet of little caramel-dipped cream puffs (choux buns) — a worthy tribute to the patron saint of pâtissiers?

If caviar is your idea of the ultimate in luxury, Caviar Kaspia is almost next door, cheek by jowl with La Maison de la Truffe. Here, you can take a seat at a sidewalk table overlooking the Madeleine church and experience a taste of heaven in a dégustation of truffles with Champagne. If all this is beyond your budget, just wander in and breathe in the heady aroma of fresh white and black "diamonds". Offset the earthy richness at the Japanese pâtisserie next door, which transports you to the Orient with an exquisite array of artistic cakes and pastries.

In gastronomic terms, the place de la Madeleine equals the area's luxury shops. But it offers another hidden delight. To the right of the church entrance, just before the colorful little flower market in the center of the square, a spiral staircase leads down to Paris's most opulent public lavatory — a 1905 extravaganza of art deco carved mahogany cubicles with stained-glass windows, a floral ceramic ceiling, and an imperial throne where you can sit to have your shoes shined.

For splendor, the lavish Opéra de Palais Garnier would be hard to beat. It was once the largest theater in the world and dominates the place de l'Opéra. Its architect, Charles Garnier, also designed the opulent Café de la Paix opposite, where you can sit and watch la vie parisienne go by over a cup of staggeringly expensive coffee. For a cheaper option, with a vast terrace overlooking the Opéra, the Printemps department store has a self-service restaurant on the ninth floor. It may lack some of the elegance, but the views are stunning.

Boutique Maille

Maille have been making mustard since 1747 and this little boutique, tucked away in a corner of the place de la Madeleine, is a veritable shrine to the condiment. Over thirty varieties of mustard ensure that you'll find the right one to go with any dish. Choose from perennial favorites (Dijon, whole grain, green herb) or try one of the seasonal specials like fig and coriander or crystalized orange and ginger. You can taste before you buy, and choose between standard jars, gorgeous hand-decorated china pots, and create-your-own gift packs. There is also a range of flavored oils, vinegars, and piquant cornichons.
6 PLACE DE LA MADELEINE,
01 40 15 06 00

Caviar Kaspia

The exceptional range of caviars at this little boutique costs less than at Fauchon, but if they are still out of your price range, try the superb smoked salmon with fresh blinis, or go for humbler but delicious smoked sturgeon, trout, herrings, or sprats. Caviar Kaspia boasts the biggest selection of vodkas in Paris — drink enough and you'll forget the price of the caviar.
17 PLACE DE LA MADELEINE,
01 42 65 66 21

Dallayou

This branch of the self-styled "ambassador of the art of catering" supplies sumptuous traiteur dishes to the Elysée Palace and nearby embassies, and to ordinary folk who patronize their shop. Treat yourself to a takeout feast with ready-prepared medallions of lobster with ceps, pheasant terrine, and ambrosial *gâteau Opéra* (an almondy sponge with dark

Fauchon

Fauchon was founded in 1886 by a grocer from Normandy named Auguste Félix Fauchon. He started selling fine foods from a cart on the place de la Madeleine and a year later he opened his own fine foods store. From these humble origins today's emporium was born. Even the doorman outside Fauchon's iconic emporium is smartly dressed in the store's distinctive black-and-white livery with flashes of vivid pink. The interior of the shop has had a minimalist revamp; it has lost some of its former extravagant pizzazz, but the window displays remain as spectacular as you'll find anywhere, with stunning arrays of exotic fruit and vegetables, crystalized fruits, chocolates, palate-tingling charcuterie and drool-inducing pâtisserie. Inside, you'll find teas, jams, foie gras, and every kind of luxury food, plus a new and expensive wine section. The beautifully packaged gift boxes would send any foodie into paroxysms of joy.
26–30 PLACE DE LA MADELEINE, 01 47 42 60 11

Maison de la Truffe

From October to March, truffle-lovers will find paradise in the form of the fresh black Périgord and white Italian truffles, whose intense aroma pervades this little shop. The rest of the year they will have to content themselves with truffles in myriad forms — preserved in jars and tins, inserted into duck and goose foie gras and cheeses, flavoring pâtés and terrines, oils, vinegars, bottled sauces, and condiments. If you can turn your mind away from truffles, there is a fine selection of caviar, jams, and wines.
19 PLACE DE LA MADELEINE,
01 42 65 53 22

chocolate ganache and coffee buttercream), le Dallayou with almond praline, or their famous macaroons. Dishes change with the season, and there is always a range of interesting charcuterie, smoked salmon, foie gras, and breads. If you prefer to eat sur place, there's a tearoom upstairs.
101 RUE DU FAUBOURG ST-HONORÉ,
01 42 99 90 00

Hédiard

The scale is more intimate at Hédiard than at Fauchon, but it has also been updated to give the impression of an extremely upmarket souk. Hédiard has been selling its range of teas and coffees since 1850. A huge coffee grinder dominates the back of the shop, and the divine aroma of freshly ground coffee and leaf teas pervades the establishment. Unusual jams include sweet pink potato or rosehip varieties, and there's a staggering range of exotic fresh fruits. Edible and non-edible gifts like flavored oils and spice-scented candles are wrapped in Hédiard's signature red-and-black stripes.
21 PLACE DE LA MADELEINE,
01 43 12 88 88

Hévin

The welcome is cool at Jean-Paul Hévin's ultra-chic rue St-Honoré boutique, but the quality of his chocolates makes a visit worthwhile. Maître Hévin honed his skills in Japan and the Asian influence is evident in the flavorings he uses, like ginger and smoked tea. For the adventurous, try the "Dynamic Collection" of aphrodisiac chocolates scented with sultry spices, or cheese-filled chocolates, designed to start or finish a meal.
231 RUE ST-HONORÉ,
01 55 35 35 96

Ladurée

The original Ladurée, founded in 1862, still outshines its upstart sibling on the Champs-Elysées. The decadently decorated baroque shop and salon de thé has a glorious frescoed ceiling and minuscule tables and chairs which discourage long lingering teas. Better perhaps to buy the cakes and pastries to takeout. The selection of irresistibly squishy macaroons includes the divine salted caramels and seasonal specials like *cassis* (blackcurrant), chestnut, and lime with basil.
16 RUE ROYALE, 01 42 60 21 79

Lavinia

Possibly the world's largest wine store, Lavinia offers three floors of fine wines from all over the world. With a range of 1000 different spirits and 5000 wines, it's an oenophile's delight. Visit the basement for an astonishing collection of French wines including an almost priceless 1918 Mouton Rothschild, but don't be put off because you will find that prices are mostly reasonable here. The boutique on the top floor stocks wine books, glasses, and accessories. The excellent wine bar offers tastings with tapas, and the contemporary chic lunchtime restaurant doesn't charge corkage on bottles of wine purchased in the shop.
3–5 BOULEVARD DE LA MADELEINE,
01 42 97 20 20

Pages 60–1: beautifully packaged macaroons displayed in Ladurée's shop windows — irresistibly delicious.

Shops

La Maison du Miel

A little beehive of a shop selling every product imaginable from the honey bee, from flavorsome honey to candles, medicaments, and soap. Honeys are sourced from all over the world, together with those from the hives the founding Galland family tend throughout France. Their intensely flavored bronzy heather honey is world famous, as are the lime flower and lavender. Sample tastings allow you to choose your favorite.

24 RUE VIGNON, 01 47 42 26 70

La Maison du Whisky

Jean-Marc Bellier will happily bend your ear about any aspect of whisky at his little shop, which is devoted entirely to the golden nectar, with dozens of blends and single malts. The collection of 800 different labels spans the globe from Scotland to Ireland, Kentucky, Canada, Japan, and New Zealand.

20 RUE D'ANJOU, 01 42 65 03 16

Michel Cluizel

A copper fountain pouring curtains of dark, glossy chocolate entices you into Michel Cluizel's family-run shop. Everything made by this master chocolatier is of the purest chocolate, containing eighty-five to ninety-

nine percent cocoa solids. Praline-filled milk chocolate lollipops painted with cartoon animals are sheer delight for children. Grown-up chocoholics may prefer the premier cru single-estate bars, beautifully packaged chocolate assortments, or the tasting box, which takes you through every step of the chocolate-making process, from cocoa beans to cocoa butter, paste, then rich dark, creamy milk, and silky white chocolate.

201 RUE ST-HONORÉ, 01 42 44 11 66

Minamoto Kitchoan

Exotic Japanese pastries are beautifully presented at this haven of calm, which shares its premises with Caviar Kaspia. The pâtissier, Ichoshigure, combines sweet white bean paste with lotus root and ginkgo nuts, which is then wrapped in a leaf and steamed. Whole yuzu (a kind of Japanese clementine) is filled with an unctuous adzuki bean paste, and in the fall, chestnuts are candied in their skins, then enveloped in chestnut paste. Everything can be bought either to takeout or to eat in the elegant salon de thé at the back of the shop.

17 PLACE DE LA MADELEINE,
01 40 06 91 28

La Vaissellerie

Whatever you want in the way of inexpensive tableware, you'll find it at this colorful little shop crammed with painted pottery, piles of pure white Limoges porcelain plates at staggering low prices, and Fauchon china deliciously decorated with fondant-colored pastries. It's a great place for presents, with novelty items like food and wine magnets, baguette-shaped bread knives, and cheese knives with mouse motifs.

323 RUE ST-HONORÉ, 01 42 60 64 50

Lafayette Gourmet

Access this top end grocery store through the men's store adjacent to the main Galeries Lafayette for a superb selection of foods and wines. Concessions include Hédiard, Eric Kayser's wonderful breads, and Sadaharu Aoki's exquisite Japanese pastries (try the green tea or black sesame éclairs). The cheese counter stretches from here to eternity, super fresh oysters are served at the bar next to the excellent fish stall, there's a tempting display of fresh fruit and vegetables, plus standard grocery market fare — the ultimate in one-stop shopping. It's great for gifts and handy for a quick bite, with counters serving tapas, caviar, Creole, and North African dishes to eat here or takeout.

40 BOULEVARD HAUSSMANN,
01 42 82 34 56

L'Espadon, Ritz Hotel

The approach along the corridor in the legendary Ritz Hotel gives a foretaste of the opulent décor of the Espadon restaurant with its vast trompe-l'oeil ceiling, where Michel Roth presents his refined cooking. Pistachio-crusted langoustine tails come with foamy lobster sauce, spit-roasted wild duck is accompanied by caramelized roast figs and carved at the table, and the turbot cooked whichever way you choose and served with five different sauces from silver sauceboats is an experience to cherish. To drink, choose, if you can, from more than a 1000 bottles of wine. In fine weather you can eat in the ravishing lushness of the courtyard garden. The service is not over formal and men can dispense with their jackets at lunchtime (although they are de rigueur in the evening). Prices are high — this is the Ritz after all — but there's a bargain set lunch.

15 PLACE VENDÔME, 01 43 16 30 80

Androuët sur le Pouce

For cheese-lovers, this is the ultimate fast food (*sur le pouce* means "a quick bite") with a difference. Gone is the old-fashioned indigestion-inducing menu where every course consisted of cheese. In its place is a cheerful casual bar serving tartines (open sandwiches), or tasting platters of cheese, smoked fish, and charcuterie. Choose five, seven or — if you are a cheese-oholic — fifteen different cheeses from a selection of dozens, accompanied by excellent bread and salad and a great choice of wines. Finish with — what else — a slice of deliciously creamy cheesecake.

49 RUE ST-ROCH, 01 42 97 57 39

L'Ardoise

The décor is basic and the tables a little too close for comfort at this little bistro, but the inventive cooking and reasonable prices ensure that it's always packed, particularly on Sundays, when most restaurants in the area are closed. Oysters with small sausages, herb-encrusted lamb tournedos, and home-cooked duck foie gras are always reliable and attractively presented. Desserts include an impeccable rum baba and creamy, rich petits pots of mascarpone and chocolate cream.

28 RUE DE MONT THABOR,
01 42 96 28 18

Restaurants in Faubourg St-Honoré, Madeleine & Opéra

Café de la Paix

Charles Garnier's Second Empire décor justifies the exorbitant prices at this landmark Paris brasserie right opposite the architect's opulent opera house. It's worth the price to sit on the elegant fin-de-siècle terrace (glassed-in in the colder months) with a cup of coffee and a generously filled baguette and watch Parisian life go by. Don't expect a full-frontal view of the Opéra; the terrace is sideways-on to the magnificent building.

12 BOULEVARD DES CAPUCINES, 01 40 07 30 20

Le Carré des Feuillants

Step through the gracious courtyard to enter this elegant wood-paneled restaurant, once a seventeenth-century convent. The ambience is sober and formal and service follows suit, but the food sparkles as brightly as the splendid Murano crystal chandeliers. Alain Dutournier is intensely proud of his native Gascony and refines the cuisine of the region in dishes like minuscule baby squid with pipérade and Espelette pepper, veal sweetbreads with oyster jus, and grilled turbot with quinoa and morels. Delicate scallops are wrapped in featherlight puff pastry and served with contrastingly earthy cabbage and truffles. Desserts such as pistachio cream with candied tangerines or Jubilee cherries with baby chocolate baba are fabulously inventive, and wines from south-western France help keep the price of the meal in check.

14 RUE DE CASTIGLIONE, 01 42 86 82 82

Cuisine et Confidences

On a fine day, choose an outside table at this friendly modern café/bar, where cheerful red blankets are provided to keep off the chill. Quirky names don't detract from the quality of the inventive food, and portions are enormous. *L'Egoiste* is a whole duck foie gras in a glass pot, there's half a cow's worth of steak tartare, and *les Aventures de Rabbi Jacob*, a mammoth corned beef, turkey, and pickle sandwich, wouldn't disgrace a New York deli. Freshly made substantial salads like *Par Faim des Femmes* are less calorific options, with tangy tomato and creamy eggplant (aubergine) purées, sun-dried tomatoes, mozzarella, and Parmesan. Finish with a delicious tarte Tatin. The cozy red wine bar upstairs is a popular after-work venue.

33 PLACE DU MARCHÉ ST-HONORÉ, 01 42 96 31 34

L'Evasion

You may have to fight to get a table at this hugely popular wine bar, where organic wines play a starring role. A glass of Burgundy goes down well with a chunk of superb *jambon persillé* (parsleyed ham terrine) from the same region, or perhaps some salami or Parma ham with a crisp Chablis. For hungry drinkers, the blackboard menu offers more substantial fare like veal kidneys à la moutarde or lamb steaks, with cheese or Berthillon ice creams to finish.

7 PLACE ST-AUGUSTIN, 01 45 22 62 20

La Luna

Unexpectedly located in a quiet residential street behind the Gare St-Lazare, La Luna is not easy to find. Don't be confused by the name "*Les Années Trente*" etched on the huge glass frontage; the 1930s windows are protected and can't be changed, but the fish on the blue awning above gives a clue to the delights within. The plain décor belies the superlative quality of the fish, which is presented whole at the table before being cooked to order. Portions are huge — a whole turbot is intended for two — and preceded by a complimentary bowl of clams, which is almost a meal in itself. Don't stint on the buttery *pommes mousseline* (creamy mashed potatoes), but leave room for a rum-soaked baba filled with a volcano of pastry cream and a bottle of old rum for you to help yourself — each baba is big enough for four.

69 RUE DU ROCHER, 01 42 93 77 61

Le Meurice, Hôtel Meurice

Star chef Yannick Alleno offers contemporary two-star cooking in the superbly elegant nineteenth-century surroundings of the Hôtel Meurice. With the lightest of touches, he extracts every ounce of flavor from top-notch ingredients and creates unexpected combinations. Scallops are dressed with balsamic vinegar and served with a trembling hazelnut bavarois; the richness of crab is offset with tangy citrus fruit and mellowed with herb cream and caviar. Finish with a towering millefeuille assembled at the table.

228 RUE DE RIVOLI, 01 44 58 10 10

Le Pain Quotidien

Parisians have embraced the idea of brunch and this branch of the popular Belgian chain is always heaving at weekends, when people in search of a good value meal form queues to eat at the convivial communal tables. Breakfasts offer buttery croissants, delicious breads, a selection of spreads from chocolate to nutty and jam, with organic yoghurts, free-range eggs, bacon, and sausages. Lunches and brunches are table d'hôte, with enormous salads and tartines. The counter inside sells bread, baked goods, and jams to takeout.
18 PLACE DU MARCHÉ ST-HONORÉ,
01 42 96 31 70

Le Soufflé

The idea of a meal based entirely on soufflés may seem de trop, but the concept works wonderfully well at this little restaurant tucked away behind the rue de Rivoli. Choose from a dozen or so savory versions, including spinach, wild mushroom, Roquefort or seafood, or variations on the theme, with mini-soufflés set atop a salmon escalope. Two soufflés (first and main courses) might seem enough, but the sugary aroma of seductively high-rise edifices like apple and Calvados, chocolate with dark chocolate sauce, and historic Grand Marnier is too good to resist. If soufflés really aren't your thing, succulent roast lamb and other alternatives are available. The excellent value prix-fixe lunch offers a salad, two soufflés, wine, and coffee at a very affordable price.
36 RUE DE MONT THABOR,
01 42 60 27 19

Angélina

The décor of the legendary Rumpelmayer's Viennese tearoom has been marginally modernized, but Paris's premier salon de thé still has the old-world feel of the days when Marcel Proust and Coco Chanel came to take tea. Service can be surly, but put up with it for the famous *chocolat Africain* — a steaming cup of rich, dense chocolate ceremoniously brought on a silver tray with extra airy whipped cream to gild the lily. Pastries are good, but the star is the Mont Blanc, a creation of chewy meringue topped with sweet chestnut purée and a mound of whipped cream.
226 RUE DE RIVOLI, 01 42 60 82 00

Filets de Turbot au Beaujolais

Fillets of turbot with red wine sauce

As you might expect, the cooking in this area of Paris makes use of the most expensive ingredients. Turbot is the king of fish, with a rich, meaty texture that combines brilliantly with a full-bodied gamay wine. If you can get it, brill is a little cheaper than turbot and works equally well, but don't stint on the wine — use the best Beaujolais Villages you can afford (drinking the rest of the bottle will be a pleasure).

SERVES 4

PREPARATION TIME: 10 MINUTES

COOKING TIME: 15 MINUTES

4 fillets of turbot or brill, 175–200g/6–7oz each, skinned	110g/4oz/1 cup thinly sliced shallots
salt and freshly ground white pepper	200ml/7fl oz/⅞ cup robust red wine (preferably Beaujolais Villages)
150g/5oz/⅔ cup butter, chilled and diced, plus extra for greasing	200ml/7fl oz/⅞ cup fish stock

Preheat the oven to 180°C/350°F/gas mark 4. Season the fish on both sides. Generously butter a deep flameproof dish large enough to hold the fillets in one layer without overlapping. Scatter the shallots over the bottom and lay the fillets on top. Pour in the wine and fish stock, cover the dish and bring the liquid to just below boiling point. Place in the oven and bake for 6–8 minutes, until the fish is just cooked.

Carefully lift out the fillets and put them on a large plate. Cover with foil and keep warm. Put the dish over a high heat, bring the liquid to a boil and cook until it has reduced by half. Whisk in the butter, one piece at a time, to make a smooth, glossy sauce. Season to taste. Divide the shallots among four warmed plates and lay the fish on top. Pour the sauce over and around the fish.

Champignons Sauvages à la Persillade

Wild mushrooms with garlic and parsley

In the fall, Parisian markets are full of glorious wild mushrooms, and you'll find them featured on almost every restaurant menu. Chanterelles and ceps are particularly delicious cooked *à la persillade*, but you can substitute any wild mushrooms, or, if you prefer, use a mixture.

SERVES 4

PREPARATION TIME: 10 MINUTES

COOKING TIME: 15 MINUTES

1kg/2¼lb chanterelles, ceps, or other wild mushrooms	40g/1½oz/2 cups fresh flat-leaf parsley, leaves only
salt and freshly ground black pepper	2 tbsp olive oil or goose fat
3–4 garlic cloves	sourdough bread, to serve

Cut off the earthy ends of the mushroom stalks and either wipe the caps with a damp cloth or wash them very briefly under a trickle of cold water. Halve the mushrooms (quarter them if they are very large) and sprinkle with a little salt and pepper.

Peel and finely chop the garlic. Finely chop the parsley leaves and mix them with the garlic. Heat the oil or goose fat in a large skillet (frying or sauté pan), add the mushrooms, and sauté over a high heat for approximately 5 minutes. Give an occasional stir with a wooden spatula, but be careful not to break up the mushrooms.

Lower the heat and cook for another 5 minutes, until the mushrooms are tender, then stir in the parsley and garlic, season, and cook for another minute or two. Serve with lightly toasted sourdough bread.

The Ritz Escoffier Cooking School

Where better to learn the art of French cooking than in Paris? And what more glamorous location could there be than the kitchens of the Ritz Hotel, an eighteenth-century hôtel particulier, on the beautiful place Vendôme? The Ritz is the only grand hotel in Paris that gives the public a chance to share the culinary secrets and savoir-faire of its chefs.

When César Ritz opened his eponymous Paris hotel in 1898 and persuaded the greatest ever culinary genius, Auguste Escoffier, to become his head chef, a legendary partnership and *art de vivre* (art of living) were created. Escoffier is acknowledged to be the father of modern gastronomy and his *Guide Culinaire* is still considered the "bible" of culinary arts, so it's surprising that it was ninety years before the Ritz instituted a cooking school in his name. The school is open to any gastronome of any age, from children and complete beginners to would-be professional chefs.

Naturally, there are courses on classical French cuisine (Escoffier would turn in his grave if there were not), but you can choose to learn virtually any cooking or entertaining skill you care to name, from pastry- and bread-making to seafood, chocolate, festive feasts, food and wine pairing, even flower arranging. If you can't think what to cook on the weekend, there are Saturday workshops focusing on seasonal specialties, so you can learn how to whip up a humble crumble (a current French passion) or bring a little luxury home with sea scallops, foie gras, or truffles.

Deep in the bowels of the hotel, across the corridor from the world-famous kitchen, you'll find the two training areas. The tiled wall of the demonstration room is adorned with a beautiful but faintly grisly still life depicting a stag's head and a collection of dead game birds. Vegetarians or the squeamish might do better to concentrate on the state-of-the-art navy-and-copper workstation where every Monday afternoon a Ritz chef shares the secrets of his craft. If it's a pastry day, he'll prepare a raft of mouthwatering desserts with seasonal fruits (perhaps delicious pastry purses with glorious purple figs and quinces in season), souffléd crêpes and crisp, creamy vanilla millefeuille, before plating them up with inimitable panache and inviting the drooling audience to tuck in. Once you have learnt the secret of making perfect puff pastry (Ritz chefs use slabs of "dry" butter, which has an eighty-two percent or greater fat content) and discovered the art of creating crisp leaves of millefeuille (pop a baking sheet on top of the pastry before baking), you may never be tempted to use shop-bought pastry again. Demonstrations are in French, but an assistant gives a simultaneous translation and students are encouraged to question the chef or comment on the proceedings.

The second training kitchen is more hands-on, and designed for would-be professional chefs. A six-week course leads to a César Ritz Diploma, but it takes thirty weeks of hard work to attain the coveted Ritz Escoffier Superior Diploma and the chance to work in the Ritz kitchens, preparing food for the double-Michelin-starred Espadon restaurant. And if you believe in starting young, there are courses for kids, where *"les petits marmitons du Ritz"* (little chef's assistants) can have fun learning how to prepare a picnic, make chocolate rabbits for Easter, or roast a wild duck for a special Mother's Day lunch.

Pintade Laqué aux Figues

Honeyed guinea hen with figs

The combination of honey and figs gives a wonderful sweetness to the guinea hen. French guinea fowl tend to be fatter and more succulent than other varieties, so if you can buy one in Paris, you might make it stretch to six servings.

SERVES 4
PREPARATION TIME: 5 MINUTES
COOKING TIME: 1 HOUR

1.5kg/3¼lb guinea hen
salt and freshly ground
   white pepper
4 sprigs of fresh rosemary
2 sprigs of fresh thyme
25g/1oz/2 tbsp butter, softened
2 tbsp clear honey
8 fresh purple figs

2 tbsp Cointreau
juice of 3 oranges
25g/1oz/2 tbsp unsalted butter,
   diced

Preheat the oven to 180°C/350°F/gas mark 4. Season the guinea hen inside and out with salt and freshly ground pepper, put the herbs in the cavity, and smear the breast with the softened butter. Put the bird into a roasting pan and roast in the oven for about 30 minutes, basting occasionally.

Drizzle half the honey over the guinea hen. Halve the figs and arrange them, cut-side up, around the guinea hen in the roasting pan. Return it to the oven for about 20 minutes, until the bird's juices run clear when you pierce the thickest part of the thigh with a skewer. Remove the figs from the pan and keep them warm. Drizzle the rest of the honey over the the top of the bird and return it to the oven for a few minutes to give the finished dish an attractive glaze.

Take the pan out of the oven, transfer the guniea hen to a cutting board, and place the pan over a medium heat. Pour in the Cointreau, add the orange juice, and scrape up the sediment from the bottom of the pan. Pass the juices through a sieve into a saucepan, heat gently, and whisk in the diced butter. Season to taste.

Cut the bird into 6–8 pieces, place on a serving dish, and pour the sauce over. Arrange the roasted figs around the edge and serve.

Crêpes Roxelane

In this classic recipe from the Ritz Hotel, the crêpes are filled
with an unctuous Chiboust cream, which rises like a soufflé. For
a contrast of flavors and textures, decorate them with chopped
pistachios and serve with a fresh raspberry or strawberry coulis,
made by puréeing 150g/5oz/1 cup of raspberries or strawberries
with 50g/2oz/½ cup of superfine (caster) sugar and a tablespoon
of lemon juice.

SERVES 4
PREPARATION TIME: 20 MINUTES
COOKING TIME: 10 MINUTES FOR THE CREPES, PLUS 5 MINUTES FOR
THE FINISHED DISH

CREPE BATTER:

100g/3½oz/¾ cup all-purpose
   (plain) flour
pinch of salt
25g/1oz/2 tbsp superfine
   (caster) sugar
2 large eggs
1½ tbsp sunflower or peanut
   oil, plus extra for cooking
250ml/9fl oz/1 cup milk
25g/1oz/2 tbsp butter, melted
   and cooled

TO SERVE:

confectioners' (icing) sugar
   chopped pistachios
   (optional)
red fruit coulis, to serve
   (optional)

CHIBOUST CREAM:

500ml/18fl oz/2 cups milk
100g/3½oz/½ cup superfine
   (caster) sugar
½ vanilla bean (pod), split
   lengthwise
50g/2oz/¼ cup unsalted butter
6 large eggs, separated
25g/1oz/¼ cup all-pupose
   (plain) flour, sifted
20g/¾oz/2½ tbsp cornstarch
   (cornflour), sifted
grated zest of 2 lemons

To make the crêpes, combine the flour, salt, sugar, eggs, and oil
in a bowl. Add half the milk, stir with a whisk, then stir in the
melted butter; add the rest of the milk, and whisk to a smooth
batter. Heat a crêpe pan and brush it lightly with oil. Ladle a little
batter into the center of the pan and rotate to spread it evenly over
the surface. Cook the crêpe for about 1 minute on each side until
golden, tossing or turning it with a palette knife. Make a total of
eight crêpes.

To make the Chiboust cream, bring the milk to a boil with half
the sugar, the vanilla bean, and the butter. In a bowl, beat the egg
yolks with the remaining sugar until frothy, then whisk in the sifted
flour and cornstarch, ladling in the milk little by little as you whisk.
Pour the mixture back into the saucepan and cook, whisking
vigorously, until it becomes a thick custard. Boil for 1 minute, pour
the custard into a shallow dish, cover with plastic wrap, and leave
to cool. Stir the lemon zest into the cooled custard. Beat the egg
whites until stiff and gently fold them into the custard with a
rubber spatula.

Preheat the oven to 200°C/400°F/gas mark 6. Lay the crêpes
flat on the work surface and pipe or spread about 2 tablespoons
of the Chiboust cream along the center. Roll them up loosely,
place them on a greased baking sheet, and cook in the oven for
4–5 minutes until the filling has puffed up. Put two crêpes on each
serving plate, dust with confectioners' sugar, sprinkle with
pistachios, and serve with red fruit coulis, if you like.

Landmarks

Once you have enjoyed the gourmet shops in place de la Madeleine, you'll still have some time to take in the cultural delights of the area. Relish the superb view from La Madeleine — an immense neo-classical church and one of the city's most famous landmarks — then walk down rue Royale to place de la Concorde, and across the river to the Palais Bourbon, home of the Assemblée Nationale (the French parliament). Nearby, you will find one of Paris's oldest and most attractive public gardens, the Tuileries, and one of the world's most sumptuous theatres, and for a time its largest, the Opéra de Palais Garnier. If all this richness makes you hungry, Paris's finest food shops are just across the square.

Jardin des Tuileries

If you are suffering from cultural indigestion, the Tuileries offer a relaxing haven. Named after the medieval tile factories that once stood on the site, the symmetrical gardens were laid out in the seventeenth century and have been the most fashionable place for a Parisian promenade ever since. It's delightful to walk along the gravel pathways past immaculate lawns, colorful box-hedged flowerbeds, and ponds with fountains, and to admire or puzzle over the modern sculptures interspersed with the original ornamental statuary. The gardens are great for children, with donkey rides, an old fashioned carousel in summer, and a large pond where kids of all ages sail old-fashioned wooden toy boats rented from the adjacent stall. It's the perfect place for a picnic, to buy an ice cream, or patronize one of the cafés.

La Madeleine

The place de la Madeleine is dominated by this colossal neo-classical church. Building began in 1764, but it wasn't consecrated until 1845. In the intervening years, attempts were made to transform it into a bank, a railway station, parliament buildings — and, most grandiose of all, Napoleon ordered it to be made into a "temple of glory" dedicated to his armies. To this end, fifty-two giant Corinthian columns supporting a triangular pediment complete with sculpted frieze were added to make it resemble a Greek temple. The lavish marble-and-gilt interior is topped with three vast cupolas, and the pseudo-Grecian side chapels are faced with multicolored marble. It makes a suitably grand setting for society weddings and for funerals, which have included those of Frédéric Chopin and Marlene Dietrich.

Opéra de Palais Garnier

The Opéra de Palais Garnier was designed by the then unknown architect Charles Garnier, who beat more than 170 contenders in a competition to design a "temple for art with divinity". His design did not meet with royal approval; the king's reaction on seeing a model of the building was: "What is this style? It's not a style. It's not Greek, it's not Louis XVI," to which Garnier scornfully replied: "Those styles have had their day. This style is Napoleon III, and you complain?"

Inaugurated in 1875, the opera house proved to be a model of overblown Second Empire architecture, with its wedding-cake facade festooned with sculptures of music and dance, provocative torch-bearing nymphs, and Apollo topping the spectacular copper dome.

The inside is equally extravagant, its lavish baroque foyer and splendid marble-and-gilt staircase leading to the horseshoe-shaped auditorium, which can hold 2,200 spectators. The opulent red-and-gold décor is enhanced by a huge crystal chandelier and by the ceiling, painted by Marc Chagall with scenes from opera and ballet. Nowadays most operas are performed in the far less exotic Opéra Bastille, and the Opéra Garnier is almost exclusively devoted to ballet.

Place Vendôme

For a glimpse into how the rich live, venture into the elegant classical place Vendôme, lined with exclusive jewelry shops frequented by moneyed residents and clients of the prestigious Ritz Hotel, where Diana, Princess of Wales, ate her last supper before her fateful car journey in 1997. Busloads of tourists still come to gawp at the many celebrities who stay at the Ritz. But often they miss the true glory of the square, commissioned in 1685 by Louis XIV and designed by the architect Jules Hardouin-Mansart. The centerpiece was a proud equestrian statue of the king. Inevitably a revolutionary mob destroyed it, and it was replaced by the iconic 144-foot-high column encased in bronze, cast from 1,250 cannons captured at the Battle of Austerlitz in 1805 and crowned with a statue of Napoleon Bonaparte (who else?) dressed as Caesar, complete with a laurel wreath.

Pages 74–5: the sumptuously decorated Opéra de Palais Garnier, designed by Charles Garnier in the late nineteenth century as a "monument to art, to luxury, to pleasure".

Les Halles & Louvre

(1st, 2nd & 3rd arrondissements)

For art and culture lovers, nowhere in Paris can match the Louvre art gallery, with its stupendous collection of paintings, sculpture and artefacts — one of the finest in the world. You could easily spend a week, a month, a year, or even a whole lifetime visiting the museum without seeing everything displayed in it. The exhibits cover a vast period from about 7000 BC to 1848 and there are 35,000 works on display. If all this leaves you feeling a little overawed, find comfort in one of the many nearby cafés or bistros.

Les Halles & Louvre
(1st, 2nd & 3rd arrondissements)

The construction of I. M. Pei's Pyramid (below) in the center of the Louvre may have been controversial, but without the building works needed for President Mitterand's *Grand Projet du Louvre*, the medieval origins of the palace might never have been uncovered. It started life as a twelfth-century hunting lodge — the name may derive from the Latin *luperia* ("wolf lodge") — for Philippe-Auguste. Before setting off for the Crusades, the prudent king constructed a fortress and dungeon to protect the right bank of the Seine, the remains of whose massive walls are now exposed to view in floodlit glory in the Sully wing of the museum. Two centuries later, Charles V moved his court to the old fortress and embarked on transforming it into a palace with all the attendant trappings of luxury and power. Alas for the king and his courtiers, the stench from the ditches and the old dungeon during the building works was often unbearable and the court was frequently forced to decamp. Eventually, the sixteenth-century king François I demolished Philippe Auguste's twelfth-century fortress-cum-dungeon and replaced it with the grandiose Renaissance palace that we know today. He launched the Louvre's art collection, bringing the *Mona Lisa* and its creator, Leonardo da Vinci, to France. Napoleon continued the

tradition, filling the museum with artworks plundered during his military campaigns, although these were returned to their rightful owners in 1815.

The museum has no shortage of eateries. No matter where you are, when you are sated with works of art, you can find a nearby café for some refreshment. The Denon and Richelieu cafés both have summer terraces, but children will probably prefer the basement l'Universelle Resto in the galerie du Carrousel, a self-service restaurant where they can pick and mix food from around the world, from Lebanese, Mexican, and Italian, to burgers and crêpes. If your taste is a little more sophisticated, take a seat on the terrace of the Café Marly overlooking the Pyramid and relax with a cup of coffee or a glass of wine while you take in the view.

When you are exhausted from your visit to the Louvre, one of the most pleasant places to relax is in the tranquil Jardin du Palais Royal. Filled with beautiful trees and colorful flowerbeds, the garden is surrounded by elegant eighteenth-century arcades housing offbeat art galleries, quirky shops and a sprinkling of cafés. Choose carefully which one you patronize because inevitably some are tourist traps. The Cour d'Honneur comes as something of a culture shock amid the eighteenth-century refinement, with its controversial modern addition of black-and-white-striped columns of different heights and a fountain filled with shiny steel balls like futuristic scoops of ice cream.

For more traditional elegance, walk up the rue Vivienne towards the Bourse and duck into the fashionable Galerie Vivienne, one of a network of elegant covered galleries built in the nineteenth century as a sort of stylish

precursor to shopping malls. It's worth a detour to admire the impressive architecture of the gallery, but it's a good place to feed the body as well as the mind. There's a great wine merchant here, along with a welcoming salon de thé and a restaurant.

Seven centuries before the Galeries were built, a network of covered markets sprang up in les Halles, Paris's original wholesale food market, later aptly dubbed the "stomach of Paris" by the writer Emile Zola. From their humble beginnings in 1181, les Halles never stopped growing in importance. Businessmen and merchants made their fortunes and built themselves splendid mansions in the market area, and in the mid-nineteenth century, splendiferous glass-and-cast-iron pavilions were erected to house the market stalls. Sadly, when the market was relocated to suburban Rungis in 1969, the pavilions were demolished and for years nothing remained in les Halles but a cavernous hole in the ground, which was finally filled by the dismal and much loathed Forum des Halles.

New plans are afoot to improve the area, but they may not come to fruition for years. Meanwhile, the stomach of Paris is almost empty, although a few of the old market bistros remain, most notably the iconic Au Pied de Cochon, which is open day and night and serves as a reminder of the once-bustling market life of a once-vibrant area.

Pages 76–7: the innovative and ultra-modern steel-ball sculpture and fountain created by Belgian artist Pol Bury is set in the center of the courtyard of the Palais Royal.

79

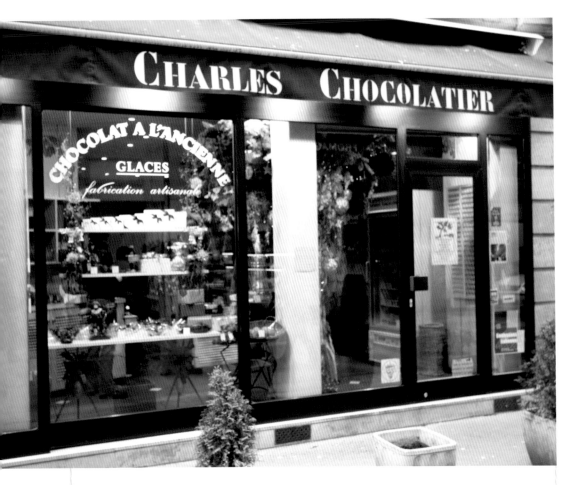

Charles

Since 1900, the family has been making chocolates *à l'ancienne* (traditionally), without animal fats — no cream or butter — so you'll find nothing but the richest, darkest assortment of chocolates containing only cocoa butter to let the true flavor and aroma sing out. Sink your teeth into the *bûche à la praliné*, an unbelievably gorgeous chocolate log studded with hazelnuts and pistachios, keep cool with home-made ice cream, or escape the cold with a cup of steaming dark hot chocolate — you'll be tempted to throw away the bathroom scales for ever.

15 RUE MONTORGUEIL, 01 45 08 57 77

A. Simon

Porcelain plates, platters, and dishes, salt and pepper mills, mixing bowls and terrines are cheek by jowl with cheese wires, paper doilies, and frills for lamb chops in this century-old professional kitchenware shop. Elegant additions to the dinner party table include wine tags and menu cards, plus wicker cheese trays and bread baskets. The annex across the courtyard stocks professional cookware.

36 RUE ETIENNE MARCEL, 01 42 33 71 65

E. Dehillerin

Every possible item of cookware that any cook's heart could desire can be found in this chaotic shop, where an entire batterie de cuisine covers every surface, including the ceiling. From a massive copper turbot kettle to a single skewer, you'll find it here amid the clutter of tartlet pans, strainers, silicone bakeware, knives and tools for sharpening them, and a host of utensils you never dreamt of. Step over the piles of pots and pans to find an assistant — what they lack in charm, they make up for in encyclopedic knowledge of where to find what you want amid the disorder.

18–20 RUE COQUILLIÈRE, 01 42 36 53 13

Kioko

If you fancy a change from French food, join the queue of homesick students at this Japanese grocery store and traiteur for a world of teas, saké, and Japanese delicacies like shrimp paste and bonito flakes. Takeout fresh sushi and authentic ready-prepared dishes from the traiteur counter, or eat them in the shop.

46 RUE DES PETITS-PÈRES, 01 42 61 33 66

Legrand Filles et Fils

This paradise for wine lovers, one of the oldest grocer and wine merchant in France, spans the Galerie Vivienne, with cellars stretching underneath the gallery. On one side there's a shop selling wine accoutrements — unusual corkscrews, tasting glasses, decanters, and books about wine: everything from vine to bottle. The wine store on the other side, retains its 1880s elegance and offers a superb selection of more than 4000 wines, many from little-known producers, with knowledgeable staff to help you make your choice. Sample before you buy at the *espace-dégustation* (tasting bar), or sit under the gallery roof and enjoy a glass of wine with some of the artisan foods from the grocery section.

1 RUE DE LA BANQUE, 01 42 60 07 12

La Mère de Famille

Every child's dream and a dentist's nightmare, this wonderful old-fashioned candy shop is like fairyland. Motherly assistants dispense handfuls of delicious candies from jars to the children who hurtle in on their way home from school. The shelves are crammed with every type of confectionery imaginable: lollipops, marzipan animals, chocolate teddies, ice creams, and all the old childhood favorites, alongside an unbelievable range of chocolates, fruit jellies, jams, and specialty sweets from all over France. You almost expect to see Hansel and Gretel emerging from the enormous sticky *pain d'épices* (spiced gingerbread) to join in the fun.

35 RUE DU FAUBOURG MONTMARTRE,
01 47 70 83 69

Stohrer

Since 1730, when a Polish pastry cook from the court of Louis XV opened this historic pâtisserie-cum-candyshop-cum-traiteur, Stohrer has been a favorite of Parisians and even the British Queen Elizabeth II, who visited the shop on her last official visit. History doesn't relate if she nibbled a cream-filled puff pastry crown, bit into a delectable rum baba, or munched on a mouthwatering macaroon — all the elaborate traditional pastries are superb. The traiteur offers complete ready-plated meals and an assortment of charcuterie.

51 RUE MONTORGEUIL, 01 42 33 38 20

Pages 82–3: one of the pleasantest places to relax in warmer weather with a coffee or a glass of wine is the rather handsome café at the Palais Royal.

81

Shops in Les Halles & Louvre

Poissonnerie Soguisa

The selection of fish on offer at this cheerful fish shop changes throughout the day as new stock arrives fresh from the market. If you're lucky, you may catch a bargain: the fishmongers stand in the street shouting out special offers, selling off the earlier stock at knockdown prices. Choose a lobster or live eel from the aquarium, or see what the day's catch has brought; along with sea bass, bream, and sole, there is often a great selection of Mediterranean seafood and fish.

72 RUE MONTORGEUIL, 01 42 33 05 16

MORA

This is where the professional chefs come for top quality kitchen equipment. Alongside catering-sized roasting pans, baking sheets, and baguette pans (too large for domestic ovens, so measure before you buy) keen pastry cooks and cake makers will find everything necessary for sugar and chocolate work, baking, and decorating.

13 RUE MONTMARTRE, 01 45 08 19 24

Au Panetier

The smell of fresh bread baked in the 1890 wood-fired oven draws you into this lovely belle-époque bakery, where locals flock to buy the sourdough baguettes (said to be the best in Paris), delicate milk loaves, and delicious apple tarts. Chocoholics will adore the chocolate *sablés* (fine shortbread cookies) and soft Viennese bread with chocolate chips. Lunchtime offerings include fresh pizzas and tempting sandwiches.

10 PLACE DES PETITS-PÈRES,
01 42 60 90 23

Restaurants in Les Halles & Louvre

A Priori

Whatever the weather, sit in comfortable wicker chairs and people watch while you enjoy a light lunch or cup of tea under the soaring glass roof of the Galerie Vivienne. For twenty five years, the American owner has presided over her unpretentious little tea room, serving creamy cheesecake, squidgy chocolate brownies, and comforting crumbles, and Parisians of all ages adore it. Weekend brunch offers omelets and delicious substantial salads with poached eggs, *quenelles* (fish dumplings), or sausages. But be warned: you'll have to reserve or queue for a seat, as they are hugely popular.

35–37 GALERIE VIVIENNE,
01 42 97 48 75

Bistrot Vivienne

This bustling 1900s bistro is popular with office workers and local residents, who come to enjoy the welcoming atmosphere and traditional cuisine with a twist. Steak tartare comes wittily spiked with frites, the daily special is always reliable, and fruit tarts are crisp and full of flavor. Service is friendly and efficient and the promise of a quick, inexpensive lunch is fulfilled.

4 RUE DES PETITS-CHAMPS,
01 49 27 00 50

Le Dauphin

From the outside, this family-owned 1900s brasserie looks unprepossessing, but don't be put off by appearances. The food inside is as inspirational as the outside is dull. Two Michel Guérard-trained chefs present a menu of south-western French dishes with a modern twist. First courses of goose rillettes or tuna confit with toasted country bread are made for sharing and there's a variety of inventive and traditional fish and meat dishes, with meltingly delicious pig's cheek slow-braised in Armagnac playing a starring role. Armagnac reappears in the superb prune tart, and orange tartlet comes with sticky orange sauce and orange sorbet. A modest selection of regional French wines completes the picture.

167 RUE ST-HONORÉ, 01 42 60 40 11

Le Grand Véfour

One of Paris's oldest and most opulent restaurants, Le Grand Véfour has been serving the beau monde since 1784; Napoleon and Josephine had romantic dinners à deux here. The grandeur of the magnificent mirrored dining room with its painted ceiling and paneled walls belies the charming, unstuffy service. The staff really want you to have a good time, and who would not when presented with Guy Martin's superbly executed foie gras ravioli with truffle jus or rack of lamb with coffee-chocolate sauce? Vegetables make unexpected appearances in some desserts, with pumpkin and orange sorbet, or sweet artichoke custard with candied vegetables. Ask for a table overlooking the Palais Royal gardens for a magnificent view to match the dazzling food.

17 RUE DE BEAUJOLAIS, 01 42 96 56 27

Au Pied de Cochon

This famous all-night restaurant encapsulates the spirit of the old les Halles, with hefty dishes designed to keep the market porters going until dawn. Piggy dishes abound: pig's feet, of course, and *la tentation de St-Antoine* — everything porcine from head to tail with grilled snout, ears, feet, and tail. For the faint-hearted, the *soupe à l'oignon gratinée* is legendary and the seafood is fresh. On fine days, you can eat on the terrace overlooking the Forum des Halles.

6 RUE COQUILLIÈRE, 01 40 13 77 00

Restaurants

Lemoni Café

This simple Cretan café attracts the breakfast and lunchtime crowds, who come for health-giving salads and soups made with ingredients fresh from the market every morning. Everything bursts with flavor and Mediterranean inspiration; dishes vary from day to day, but the "antioxidant salad", providing the recommended daily portions of five vegetables and two fruits, makes a regular appearance. Freshly squeezed juices enhance your well-being, and cauliflower and broccoli gratins with vegetable coulis disappear the moment they emerge from the kitchen. Come early for the pick of the crop.

5 RUE HÉROLD, 01 45 08 49 84

Au Lyonnais

This authentic 1890s lyonnais *bouchon* (modest bistro) has been given a stellar touch by superchef Alain Ducasse. The belle-époque décor remains unchanged, with decorated tiles on the walls and the original tiled floor, and wine is still served in utilitarian Duralex glasses, but who cares when the menu offers outstandingly good eggs en cocotte with langoustines, Bresse chicken with mushrooms, and superb charcuterie from Lyon? Cointreau soufflé rises to the heavens.

32 RUE ST-MARC, 01 42 96 65 04

Le Café Marly

Fashionistas adore this trendy Costes brothers' café-restaurant with its superb terrace overlooking the glass pyramid of the Louvre. When the weather is cold, it's better to sit in the cozy red-plush interior with its view over one of the museum's sculpture galleries. Come for the views or celebrity spotting, but don't expect anything better than standard modern food — smoked salmon, salads, and club sandwiches — served by beautiful, über-trendy and somewhat snooty staff.

93 RUE DE RIVOLI, 01 49 26 06 60

La Poule au Pot

One of the few remaining brasseries from the heyday of les Halles, La Poule au Pot stays open all night until six in the morning. The faded wallpaper festooned with grapes in the old-fashioned dining room has seen better days, but the food continues to please late-night diners. Traditional favorite dishes like kidneys in mustard sauce, home-made duck confit, and of course the famous chicken in a pot never lose their appeal, and chocolate délice with unctuous crème anglaise meets with approval even at 4am.

9 RUE VOUVILLIERS, 01 42 36 32 96

Villalys

Tucked in an arcade overlooking the Palais Royal gardens, amid the tourist-trap cafés, this cozy North African restaurant is a real find for an inexpensive lunch. There's always a range of reasonably priced tagines; spicing is subtle and delicious, vegetables are fresh and tasty, and portions are generous, making this a buzzing restaurant and a favorite haunt of local shop and office workers.

30 RUE DE MONTPENSIER,
01 42 61 85 99

Willi's Wine Bar

At first glance, Englishman Mark Williamson's wine bar doesn't look anything special, but pass through the corridor that runs beside the bar and you'll find out why the place is so popular. In the beamed back room, beautifully cooked and presented seasonal dishes appear from the tiny kitchen, such as caramelized onion tarte Tatin, roast cod or *rascasse* (scorpion fish), or tender venison or beef; the choice is as varied as the excellent wine list. Friendly bilingual staff will help you to choose a wine by the glass to accompany each dish to perfection.

13 RUE DES PETITS-CHAMPS,
01 42 61 03 09

Rillettes
Shredded meat

You can buy rillettes at any charcuterie, but it's fun to make your own from pork or goose. Once potted they will keep for several months, so they are a great standby. Rillettes are superb spread on lightly toasted sourdough bread, whose tangy acidity provides a perfect contrast.

SERVES 8
PREPARATION TIME: 15 MINUTES, PLUS COOLING TIME
COOKING TIME: ABOUT 3¼ HOURS

1.5kg/3¼lb pork belly, or half pork belly, half goose meat (vary the proportions according to taste)
175g/6oz/¾ cup goose fat or pork lard
1 bouquet garni (fresh thyme, rosemary, and bay leaves)
1 onion, peeled and stuck with 2 cloves
1 carrot
salt and freshly ground black pepper
6 peppercorns, crushed

Skin the pork belly and cut it and the goose meat, if you are using it, into 4 x 2-cm/1½ x ¾-inch strips. Gently melt the goose fat or lard in a heavy flameproof casserole dish. Add the meat and stir over the lowest possible heat until the fat begins to run. Add 2 tablespoons of water, the bouquet garni, onion, and carrot, increase the heat, and bring to a boil.

Lower the heat and cook very gently for 3 hours, stirring with a wooden spoon every 20 minutes or so, until the meat is tender.

Turn off the heat, remove the bouquet garni, onion, and carrot, and leave the meat to cool for about 30 minutes. When it is lukewarm, spoon off a ladleful of the fat floating on the surface and reserve it in a bowl. Mash the meat slightly with your fingertips to break up any large pieces, then use two forks to shred it. Stir thoroughly with a wooden spoon and season to taste.

Spoon the rillettes into earthenware pots or sterilized jars and leave to cool. Pour on a layer of the reserved fat to seal, sprinkle with crushed peppercorns, and leave in the fridge until completely cold. Cover with plastic wrap and keep in the fridge or freezer. The rillettes will keep for a month in the fridge or six months in the freezer until ready to serve. Once you have broken the fat seal, keep in the fridge and use within two days.

Soupe a l'Oignon Gratinée
Onion soup

This hearty soup was the classic breakfast eaten by the porters after the night shift at les Halles market. It is still served at all hours of the day and night at Au Pied de Cochon restaurant. One of the joys of this satisfying dish is the way the cheese forms strings as you spoon it from the bowl — impossible to eat elegantly!

SERVES 4
PREPARATION TIME: 10 MINUTES
COOKING TIME: 1 HOUR

75g/3oz/⅓ cup unsalted butter
700g/1½lb onions, very thinly sliced
1tsp sugar
150ml/5fl oz/⅔ cup dry white wine
2 pints/1.2 liters/5 cups good beef or chicken stock
salt and freshly ground black pepper

CROUTONS:
4 thick slices of day-old baguette or pain de campagne
200g/7oz/1¾ cups freshly grated Gruyère or Comté cheese

Melt the butter in a large saucepan, add the onions, sprinkle with sugar, and sauté for about 5 minutes until the onions begin to caramelize. Turn the heat down as low as possible and cook very gently for 20–30 minutes, until the onions are very soft and deep nutty brown. Add the wine and let it bubble for a few minutes, then pour in the stock and stir, scraping up the onions from the bottom of the pan. Bring to a boil, lower the heat, and simmer the soup for 30 minutes.

Preheat the oven to 170°C/325°F/gas mark 3. Put the bread into the oven to dry or until it is crisp and golden.

When the soup is ready, season and ladle into individual heatproof bowls or a heatproof tureen. Heat the broiler (grill) to high. Float the croûtons on top of the soup and sprinkle on the grated cheese. Place under the hot broiler until the cheese is bubbling and golden brown.

Petit Salé aux Lentilles de Puy

Salt pork with Puy lentils

Petit salé is lightly salted pork belly with a rich flavor and pretty pink-and-white coloring. It is a vital constituent of traditional hearty stews like potée and choucroûte, but it is also served sliced on navy (haricot) beans, puréed peas or, as here, lentils. A side dish of buttered cabbage provides a wonderful contrast of texture and flavor to the pork.

SERVES 6–8
PREPARATION TIME: 15 MINUTES, PLUS 1 HOUR SOAKING
COOKING TIME: ABOUT 1½ HOURS

1kg/2¼lb petit salé	1 bouquet garni, including
450g/1lb Puy lentils	a sprig of fresh thyme
1 onion, peeled and stuck	6 black peppercorns,
with 2 cloves	tied in cheesecloth
2 carrots, peeled and quartered	salt and freshly ground
2 small leeks, trimmed and	black pepper
quartered	

Soak the petit salé in cold water for about 1 hour, then drain it, place in a large saucepan, and cover with fresh cold water. Bring to a boil, skim any scum off the surface, and simmer gently for about 1 hour, until the pork is tender.

Rinse and drain the lentils. Place in a large pan, cover with cold water, then bring to a boil and simmer for 10 minutes, skimming off any scum. Drain and add the lentils to the pork with all the other ingredients. Simmer for about 35 minutes, until tender. Remove the pork and drain the lentils, reserving the cooking liquid and vegetables. Discard the bouquet garni and peppercorns. Taste the lentils and season if necessary. Put them in a warmed dish, slice the petit salé thickly and arrange on top of the lentils. Spoon over a little of the reserved cooking liquid and some of the vegetables if you like.

Pages 90–91: you'll find many traditional brasseries in Paris, which serve excellent and innovative dishes.

Iles Flottantes au Caramel

Floating islands with caramel

SERVES 4
PREPARATION TIME: 20 MINUTES
COOKING TIME: 20 MINUTES

CREME ANGLAISE (CUSTARD):	MERINGUE (ISLANDS):
4 large egg yolks	4 large egg whites
75g/3oz/scant ½ cup	95g/3½oz/½ cup superfine
superfine (caster) sugar	(caster) sugar
340ml/12fl oz/1½ cups milk	1¾ pints/1 liter/3¾ cups milk
1 vanilla bean (pod), split	
lengthwise	CARAMEL:
	110g/4oz/packed ½ cup
	superfine (caster) sugar

To make the crème anglaise, put the egg yolks and half the sugar in a bowl and whisk to a ribbon consistency. Boil the milk in a saucepan with the rest of the sugar, and the vanilla bean, then slowly pour it on to the egg mixture, whisking continuously. Return to the saucepan and heat gently, stirring continuously with a wooden spoon, until the custard is thick enough to coat the spoon. Don't let it boil, or you'll end up with scrambled eggs. Remove the vanilla bean by straining the custard into a bowl. Cover with plastic wrap and leave to cool, stirring occasionally. When it is cold, chill.

To make the meringue, whisk the egg whites to soft peaks. Add half the sugar and whisk until very stiff.

Heat the milk and the remaining sugar in a wide, shallow pan. When the milk is at simmering point, using two wet tablespoons, scoop up a quarter of the meringue, form it into an egg-shaped "island" and slide it into the milk. Repeat with the remaining meringue and poach each gently in the milk for 2 minutes. Then turn them over and poach for 2–3 minutes on the other side until just firm to the touch. Lift out with a slotted spoon and drain on kitchen towel.

To make the caramel, put the sugar in a small, heavy-bottomed saucepan and dissolve it over a low heat, stirring with a wooden spoon until it turns to a deep golden brown. Immediately take the pan off the heat.

Pour the chilled crème anglaise into individual bowls, float the meringue islands on top, and drizzle the caramel over each one.

Landmarks

This area of western Paris is not noted so much for its charm but rather its grandeur. Its greatest draw is the Musée du Louvre. With more than 35,000 exhibits, it is one of the world's greatest collections, and whether you are frustrated or overwhelmed by it, you simply can't ignore it. From here, whatever direction you head in you come across well-known sights: the peaceful Jardin du Palais Royal and Jardin des Tuileries, and the place de la Concorde with its grim history of beheadings. Finally, after experiencing all the cultural treats that the area has to offer, reward yourself with a little shopping, and perhaps a refreshing glass of wine in one of the cafés in the Galeries.

La Bourse

The Paris Stock Exchange originally had its headquarters at the Louvre before moving to the Palais Royal and then the Galerie Vivienne. In 1826, it finally found a home of its own just to the north of all three. The grandiose pseudo-Greek building was commissioned by Napoleon Bonaparte and designed by Alexandre Brongniart to resemble a temple to the great god Money. Enlarged in 1906, the trading floor was a hectic center of frantic brokering under an elaborately paneled and painted domed roof. In these days of computers, the building has outlived its useful purpose and the Bourse is due to move to new premises in 2009. And what is to become of the building? Current proposals include a new technology center and a casino.

Les Galeries

If you are caught in the rain when walking in the 2nd arrondissement, what better way to keep dry than to work your way through les Galeries? Inspired by the success of the Duc d'Orléans's shopping arcades in the Palais Royal, a network of covered galleries was built on the right bank between the eighteenth and nineteenth centuries. As shopping malls go, they were pretty impressive, with soaring glass roofs, colored floors, and ornate decorative ironwork. Of the original 140 galleries, only twenty four remain; some are just dingy reminders of a bygone age of elegance, but others have been restored to their original splendor and house chic restaurants, cafés, and shops — perfect for browsing in the dry on a wet day.

Magnificent wrought-iron gates lead into the most opulent and chic of the galleries, the 1823 Galerie Vivienne, where high fashion stores compete with a long-established bookshop, fine wine cellars, and a colorful toyshop. The heavily restored Galerie Colbert runs parallel to it and houses a rather soulless annex of the Bibliothèque Nationale, enlivened by the belle-époque Grand Colbert brasserie (noted more for its décor than its food). The passage des Panoramas is painted with circular panoramas offering the citizens of 1800 a "voyage" round the world; today it's abuzz with eateries and shops. Other passages and galleries worth visiting include the picturesque Galerie Véro-Dodat and passages Jouffroy and Verdeau.

Musée du Louvre

Many visitors to Paris are so daunted by the vast size and scale of the Louvre that they skip it altogether and miss one of the world's greatest treasure houses. The extraordinary collection spans several millennia and is spread over a vast area, with nearly twelve miles of corridors linking the three main wings. The secret is to be selective and focus on one area or exhibit at a time. It might be the *Mona Lisa*, Leonardo da Vinci's enigmatic portrait of *La Gioconda*, one of the first works collected by François I for his own delectation, and still the painting that attracts the most visitors. Other highlights are the ancient Greek *Venus de Milo* and *Winged Victory of Samothrace*, the incredible Egyptian collection, dominated by the *Great Sphinx*, paintings by all the Old Masters, and stupendous sculptures. Ever grandiose in his vision, Louis XIV intended the Louvre to be the largest museum in the world. It remains so today, and it keeps on growing.

Palais Royal

Built for Cardinal Richelieu in the seventeenth century, the palace complex originally included a theater where Molière's troupe of actors performed his plays for the cardinal and the court, including *Le Malade Imaginaire* (*The Hypochondriac*). Ironically, it was during a performance of this play that Molière collapsed and died. Later, the palace was given to Louis XIII; after his death, his widow moved in with her sons and rechristened it Palais Royal. The playboy Duc d'Orléans, Louis XIV's younger brother, enclosed the gardens with the three-storey galleries and turned them into public pleasure gardens open to all social classes, with shops, sideshows, and cafés, and elegant apartments built above the arcades. Nowadays, the Cour d'Honneur is dominated by Daniel Buren's controversial 1986 installation of black-and-white-striped columns. The palace houses the Ministry of Culture and is sadly not open to the public.

Pages 96–7: Daniel Buren's bizarrely striped columns in the Palais Royal courtyard.

Bastille & Gare de Lyon

(11th & 12th arrondissements)

When you arrive at the place de la Bastille, you might be forgiven for thinking that a minor revolution is taking place. The square and the streets radiating from it are a maelstrom of traffic, scurrying pedestrians, rollerbladers, busy shoppers, and trendy street cafés. All this innocent pleasure-making is a far cry from its darker origins. The Bastille was originally built in 1382 as a fortress (its name comes from "*bastide*" meaning "fortress") to defend the eastern gate to Paris from the proletarian rabble who lived in the suburbs and were the forebears of the revolutionaries who finally destroyed it.

Bastille & Gare de Lyon
(11th & 12th arrondissements)

The Bastille became a prison in the reign of Louis XIII, who incarcerated his enemies without evidence or trial, by means of a secret warrant called *lettres de cachet*.

Among the most famous prisoners were the writers Voltaire and the Marquis de Sade, along with the legendary Man in the Iron Mask. Prisoners were released only if they swore never to reveal what conditions were like inside the jail, which had a horrendous reputation. In reality, it was far from being uncomfortable. Meals were plentiful, portions enormous, and the wealthy could augment their diet by buying whatever luxury foods they wished. But no one can know for sure what the Bastille was like by 1789; the violent revolutionary mob who stormed the prison on July 14, 1789 razed it to the ground; nothing now remains except paving stones marking the outline.

The Bastille could scarcely be more different nowadays. After a wash and scrub-up to celebrate the bicentennial of the revolution, it has become one of the trendiest areas of Paris, with a mass of little bars, cafés, nightclubs, and restaurants. During the daytime it's a center for shopping, with music stores, fashion boutiques, and galleries selling arts and crafts; in the evening it is the place to go for a drink or a meal out, or to spend an evening at the opera in the Opéra Bastille.

The contrast between the old and new Bastille is encapsulated in the narrow, cobbled rue de Lappe. By day it used to be a hive of workshops making furniture, zinc counters, and paraphernalia for bars and brasseries; by night it was a den of thieves, where honest citizens hardly dared venture. The population came from the Auvergne, whose inhabitants were reputed to love dancing. By 1930, seventeen dubious dance halls had sprung up along the rue de Lappe, where prostitutes and pimps would dance the *frottis-frotta*, whose suggestive name needs no explanation. The most famous, le Balajo, is still there, but it's more disco than ooh-là-là now.

Lately, the rue de Lappe has acquired a less seedy reputation. It still looks rather scruffy in daylight, but at night it's a magnet for the hip young crowd, who fill its lively bars and restaurants, including La Galoche d'Aurillac at number 41, which still offers a taste of the Auvergne.

The rue du Faubourg St-Antoine is no less lively, but has a more cosmopolitan feel. Crammed with nightclubs and bars, it offers a world of entertainment from Latin America to Africa and the Caribbean. There's even an English pub and an Irish Corner.

By the time the clubs are closing, the twice-weekly Marché Bastille has sprung into life. It's the largest in Paris, extending for more than a mile along the boulevard Richard-Lenoir. On Sundays, it takes on a funfair atmosphere, with street performers, musicians, and balloon sellers entertaining the throng in the aisles between stalls selling clothes and housewares alongside fruit, vegetables, charcuterie, cheese, and fish. It's a short walk east to the cosmopolitan Marché d'Aligre, the most popular and lively of all the city's markets. Aligre is a sort of global village bursting with fruit and vegetable stalls set among genuine and not-so-genuine antiques, artefacts, crafts, and junk from North Africa and Asia.

Pages 98–9: along the riverside of the Grand Basin de l'Arsenal in the Bastille area.

Shops in Bastille & Gare de Lyon

Marché Aligre

Divided between the lovely old covered Marché Beauveau and the place d'Aligre, this buzzy cosmopolitan market is one of the cheapest and most popular in Paris. In the mornings from Tuesday through Sunday, there's a real multi-ethnic village atmosphere, with a cacophony of standholders calling out their wares, impromptu wine bars, and a wonderfully pervasive aroma of exotic herbs and spices from the mostly North African food stands. When you're overburdened with shopping bags, take a break at one of the packed, friendly cafés or order a plate of oysters with a glass of chilled white wine at Le Baron Rouge on avenue Théophile Roussel. PLACE D'ALIGRE (OFF THE RUE DU FAUBOURG ST-ANTOINE)

Chez Antoine

You'll find fine foods fit for a fiesta at this sunny southern Spanish deli, where you can get inspiration for making your own tapas or buy them already prepared. Titillate your tastebuds with spicy chorizo, tongue-tingling *soubressade* (pork sausage), and puff pastry *cocas* (turnovers). There's a fabulous range of Mediterranean charcuterie and irresistible, sweet, sticky sweetmeats like marzipan and *turrón* (nougat).
232 RUE DU FAUBOURG ST-ANTOINE, 01 43 72 21 97

attractive teapots and china. It's a great place to buy gifts — and, of course, a little something for yourself.

12 RUE DE LA ROQUETTE,
01 47 00 59 07

Marché Bastille

Clothes and housewares are crammed between the stands at this enormous Thursday and Saturday morning street market, which offers a huge choice of good value if not tip-top quality fruit and vegetables, along with Italian and Portuguese traiteurs, local cheeses, and Jacky Lorenzo's wonderful fish and seafood stall. A word of warning: the further you walk away from the place de la Bastille, the higher the prices become.

BOULEVARD RICHARD-LENOIR

Monoprix

The gourmet section of this rather downmarket grocery store sells a surprisingly comprehensive range of good quality food and wine, and is conveniently open until 12am if you are in need of a midnight feast.

97 RUE DU FAUBOURG ST-ANTOINE,
01 43 73 17 59

Pages 104–5: every day the Parisian pâtissiers prepare a dazzling display of pastries, and other delicious treats. Arrive early, because the most tempting products sell out quickly.

Gastronome

This Russian traiteur is a welcome oasis in the gastronomic desert around the Gare de Lyon. Watch the owner make fresh blinis while you peruse the shelves for jars of pickled cucumbers, marinated vegetables, and canned crab, or choose from the array of ready-prepared eggplant (aubergine) dishes, meat croquettes, and Russian salads, with a good selection of vodkas and Russian champagne to aid the entente cordiale.

26 BIS, BOULEVARD DIDEROT,
01 43 41 65 83

Maison Andraud

The enticing window display of this former pharmacy, built in 1903, is a chocoholic's dream. Inside, the wooden shelves groan with mouthwatering confectionery, top quality chocolates, whiskies, and teas, together with

Restaurants in Bastille & Gare de Lyon

Le Bistrot du Peintre

The classic 1907 interior, with bottles lined up behind the bar, and *cuisine familiale* (home cooking) make this cozy café an absolute gem. Good honest dishes like duck confit have a regional flavor, salads are generous and fresh, the wines are from the owner's property, and Berthillon ice creams are served. What more could you ask?

116 AVENUE LEDRU-ROLLIN,
01 47 00 34 39

Comme Cochons

You don't have to be piggy to eat here (*cochon* means "pig" or "pork", although *être amis comme cochons* means "to be among friends"), but you're sure to be tempted by the seasonal menus, including white asparagus with mustard sauce or fricasséed chanterelles for the first course, rich, flavorsome game stews, and regional cheeses. Dinner is a gourmet affair, but lunches are simpler, offering egg mayonnaise or charcuterie. Leave room for the heavenly moelleux au chocolat.

135 RUE DE CHARENTON,
01 43 42 43 36

La Galoche d'Aurillac

As a reminder of the days when rue de Lappe was peopled by Auvernois, this atmospheric restaurant is decorated with wooden *sabots* (clogs) and musical instruments from the Auvergne. The menu reflects the regional love for beef and cheese; carnivores can gorge on a 900-g (2-lb) steak or a plate of home-made charcuterie with traditional *aligot* (creamy puréed potatoes with aligot cheese). Packaged and tinned Auvernois products are on sale.

41 RUE DE LAPPE, 01 47 00 77 15

Les Grandes Marchés

Superchef Christian Constant oversees the menu at this smart brasserie, where striking modern décor is matched by the innovative food. Creative dishes like artichoke and celery root (celeriac) terrine, and cod with foie gras are the stars of the menu, but the traditional cuisine is not forgotten, with old brasserie favorites like thick slices of calves' liver with gratin dauphinois, and rum baba with crème Chantilly. All this combined with proximity to the Opéra doesn't come cheap.

6 PLACE DE LA BASTILLE, 01 43 42 90 32

Le Square Trousseau

Another 1900s bistro, this time located in a quiet square where time seems to have stood still. Outside tables are snapped up quickly in fine weather, but the inside, decorated in deep colors with velvet curtains and gilt mirrors, is all that a bistro should be. Dishes like garlicky terrine and steak tartare are perfectly executed and change seasonally.

1 RUE ANTOINE VOLLON, 01 43 43 00 66

Bofinger

The grandpère of belle-époque brasseries, Bofinger oozes elegance from the moment you walk through the revolving door. The opulent décor, courteous white-aproned waiters, immaculate starched tablecloths, and classic brasserie fare seem caught in a time warp. Oysters, plâteaux de fruits de mer, choucroûte, and fabulous îles flottantes are complemented by an excellent wine list. Pop upstairs for a look at the decorated dome even if you can't get a table up there. The gents' loos in the basement are a marvel of art deco ingenuity.

5–7 RUE DE LA BASTILLE,
01 42 72 87 82

Restaurants in Bastille & Gare de Lyon

Le Souk

For an authentic Moroccan eating experience, you can hardly do better than push through the tatty kelims into Le Souk, where the colorful décor and heady aromas of incense and spices transport you instantly to North Africa. Seductive first courses include b'stilla with duck, raisins, and nuts under a featherlight sugar- and cinnamon-dusted pastry lid, but the pièce de résistance are the tagines and couscous. The menu offers more than a dozen different varieties of each, all served in gargantuan portions combining rich meats, succulent vegetables, and plump dried fruits and nuts. The giant Souk couscous is a glorious combination of everything but the kitchen sink and doesn't leave room for the fresh fig millefeuille or pistachio and honey crème brûlée. The final flourish is mint tea, elegantly poured from a great height from a long-spouted teapot.

1 RUE KELLER, 01 49 29 05 08

Le Temps au Temps

Be sure to book in advance at this tiny twenty-five-seater bistro, where people flock to enjoy the creative cooking of the innovative young chef. Snail cappuccino makes an unusual first course, followed by *rascasse* (scorpion fish) with lentil and mango purée, or foie gras sautéed in red wine. Raspberry-topped sablés with caramel sauce and citrus soup with home-made madeleines are highlights of the dessert menu. Prices are amazingly reasonable for food of this quality.

13 RUE PAUL BERT, 01 43 79 63 40

Le Train Bleu

Even if you are not planning to travel south, it's worth a trip to the Gare de Lyon to experience the world's most opulent "station buffet". The food is nothing special, but who cares when you can sink into a clubby leather chair and enjoy exaggerated belle-époque mirrored splendor under a gilded ceiling with tumbling cherubs, chandeliers, and frescoes of destinations of the original *train bleu*? The classic fare evokes the glory days, with lobster salad, sole meunière, and creamy, crunchy chocolate vacherin, or rum baba.

20 BOULEVARD DIDEROT, GARE DE LYON, 01 43 43 09 06

Au Vieux Chêne

The nostalgic retro décor has been spruced up, but the charm of this ever-popular bistro remains unchanged, and the food is better than ever. Classic dishes are given an exotic touch: delicious cod steak comes with preserved lemon, and langoustine "cigars" in filo pastry are set on a bed of mango. Portions of meat are enormous, but save room for the sablés with rich chocolate mousse, or unctuous fruity desserts.

7 RUE DAHOMEY, 01 43 71 67 69

XO Extra Old Café

Drinking at this genuine old zinc bar is like stepping back into childhood. One wall is festooned with old toys, the lavatories are out of the ark, and the atmosphere is warm and amazingly lively. Students vie for sidewalk tables to enjoy burgers or steak tartare, along with low priced coffee and draft beer, and dance to the trendy music.

37 RUE DU FAUBOURG ST-ANTOINE, 01 43 71 73 45

Au Trou Gascon

If you can't afford the stellar prices at Alain Dutournier's much-lauded Carré des Feuillants off the place Vendôme, here's a chance to sample his cooking at more accessible cost. Run by his wife, Nicole, this single-Michelin-starred belle-époque restaurant offers a modern take on classic dishes from his native Gascony. They're not for the faint-hearted: foie gras, a surprisingly light version of cassoulet, and duck confit are still cholesterol-laden, but the flavors are fabulous, and the rich, darkly moist chocolate cake, and raspberry and meringue dessert are to die for. The wine list is encyclopedic and there's a choice of more than one hundred Armagnacs to help the digestion.

40 RUE TAINE, 01 43 44 34 26

Haricot d'Agneau

Leg of lamb with flageolet beans

A fine brasserie dish in which the *gigot* (leg) of lamb is cooked until meltingly tender and the delicious juices flavor the bed of beans. Use as much garlic as you like — the more, the better.

SERVES 6–8

PREPARATION TIME: ABOUT 20 MINUTES, PLUS OVERNIGHT SOAKING FOR THE BEANS

COOKING TIME: ABOUT 2¼ HOURS

1 leg of lamb, about 2kg/4½lb	flageolet beans, soaked in
salt and freshly ground	water overnight
black pepper	1 large home-made bouquet
9 garlic cloves, 1 peeled and	garni (celery, thyme, bay
cut into slivers, 8 unpeeled	leaf, and parsley)
1 large sprig of fresh rosemary	1 onion, finely chopped
75ml/3fl oz/⅓ cup olive oil	100ml/3½fl oz/½ cup
350g/12oz/2 cups dried	dry white wine

Preheat the oven to 220°C/425°F/gas mark 7. Season the lamb and make incisions into the flesh in about a dozen places. Push a sliver of garlic and a couple of rosemary needles into each incision and drizzle half the olive oil over the meat. Put it in a roasting pan and roast in the oven for 30 minutes, basting occasionally.

Lower the heat to 180°C/350°F/gas mark 4, scatter the whole unpeeled garlic cloves in the pan, and cook for another 1¼–1½ hours, until the lamb is very tender and the juices run pink when you insert a skewer into the thickest part of the meat.

Meanwhile, drain the beans and put them in a saucepan. Cover with fresh cold water, add the bouquet garni, boil for 10 minutes, then simmer for about 1 hour, until tender. Drain the beans.

When the lamb is cooked, take it out of the oven, remove from the roasting pan, and leave it to rest in a warm place.

Add the onion to the roasting pan alongside the garlic cloves, add the rest of the oil, set over a medium heat and sweat the onion until soft but not colored. Add the wine and simmer until reduced by half. Stir in the beans and simmer until hot. Remove the bouquet garni, season the beans, put them in a warmed serving dish and place the lamb on top. Carve it into thick slices at the table.

Tagine de Poulet

Chicken tagine

Of all the many ethnic cuisines in the Bastille area, my favorite is North African. I am always tempted by the aromatic colorful spices, fragrant olives, and succulent dried fruits on offer at the Algerian and Moroccan stalls at the Bastille market, where you can buy everything you need to make this tagine. Harissa paste is very hot, so add as much or as little as you like.

SERVES 4

PREPARATION TIME: 10 MINUTES

COOKING TIME: 1½ HOURS

4 *poulet fermier* (free-range)	340ml/12fl oz/1½ cups
chicken quarters	chicken stock
salt and freshly ground	1–2tsp harissa paste
black pepper	1 preserved lemon, cut into
1tbsp olive oil	large pieces
2 onions, thinly sliced	4tbsp chopped cilantro
2 garlic cloves, crushed	(coriander)
1tbsp *ras el hanout* (Moroccan	
spice mix), or 1 tsp each of	
ground cinnamon, turmeric,	
and ginger	

Cut the chicken quarters into two (thighs and drumsticks), and season them. Heat the oil in a tagine base or a large deep skillet (frying pan) with a lid, and sweat the onions and garlic for 3–4 minutes without allowing them to brown. Add the chicken to the pan, increase the heat slightly and fry, turning the chicken frequently, until evenly browned all over.

Stir in the spices, then pour in the stock, and bring to a simmer. Add harissa to taste, season if necessary, then put the lid on the tagine or skillet and simmer very gently for 1 hour. Add the preserved lemon and continue to cook, covered, until the chicken is so tender that it nearly falls off the bone.

Remove the lid from the tagine or skillet, turn up the heat and boil the liquid rapidly for a few minutes to reduce and thicken it slightly. Sprinkle the chicken with coriander and serve immediately.

Landmarks

The only visual memorial of the bloody events of the Revolution in 1789 is the towering Colonne de Juillet (July column) in the center of the square. It stands in a busy traffic circle (roundabout), a poignant reminder of France's turbulent political history, with roads leading to other squares with equally evocative names — place de la Nation and place de la République. Today, the trendy Bastille district is known for its ethnic restaurants, charming shops and galleries, hip bars and nightclubs, and the controversial Opéra de Paris Bastille, with its austere glass-and-marble facade and its expensive tickets, priced well beyond the pocket of most hard-working Parisians.

Cimetière du Père Lachaise

Vast, slightly sinister, and fascinating, Père Lachaise cemetery resembles a ghost town, with whole streets of graves and monuments arranged in higgledy-piggledy fashion and in no particular date order. You'll need a map (available at the entrance) to find the resting places of past Paris luminaries — politicians, scientists, inventors, military men, and artists — who are here in profusion. Painters include Corot, Delacroix, and Pissaro, writers are represented by Proust and Balzac (who featured Père Lachaise in his novel *Le Père Goriot*); there are also the singers Edith Piaf, Maria Callas, and Jim Morrison, whose grave remains the most visited of all. Some of the graves are utterly simple — sometimes just a plaque set into the crematorium wall — but others are gasp-inducingly grandiose. A weeping woman sits atop Chopin's tomb, while Oscar Wilde's is adorned with a massive Epstein figure of a naked Egyptian soaring to the skies. Twelfth-century tragic lovers Abelard and Eloise are finally united in a more modest grave along with poets, musicians, and the revolutionary partisan François Raspail, whose tomb resembles a prison cell.

La Colonne de Juillet

All that is left as a memorial to Paris's revolutionary past is the 164-foot-high bronze column surmounted by a gilded statue of the Spirit of Liberty, which dominates the place de la Bastille. The plinth on which it stands depicts a lion and an inscription reminding us that the column was not erected to commemorate the storming of the Bastille, but rather the 504 victims who died in a later uprising. More victims of yet another revolution were buried in the crypt in 1848.

For a time, the column shared the space with a bronze elephant fountain erected by Napoleon Bonaparte, but this was demolished in 1847. Standing alone surrounded by hectic traffic, facing the Opéra Bastille and with a fast-food joint to one side, the Colonne de Juillet is not the most impressive memorial to an event that changed France for ever.

Gare de Lyon

One of the few remaining monuments to Paris's glorious railway history, the Gare de Lyon was built at the end of the nineteenth century to replace the old landing stage where freight trains from Lyon were unloaded. Everything about the building is on a grandiose scale, from the square, turreted entrance with its four clocks to the great glass roof of the interior, and the massive nudes — Navigation, Steam, Electricity, and Mechanics — all glorifying technological progress. Modern progress continues with the introduction of the high-speed TGV trains, which connect Paris and the south of France. Above the entrance on the first floor is Le Train Bleu restaurant, a marvel of belle-époque painting and architecture. It's been

designated a historic monument, so it remains unchanged from its opening in 1901. If you fancy a taste of classic Lyonnais cuisine in grand surroundings, this is the place to come.

Opéra de Paris Bastille

Opened on July 14, 1989 for the bicentennial of the Revolution, Carlos Ott's controversial concrete and glass Bastille opera house was one of President Mitterand's *Grand Projects*, intended as a democratic contrast to the Opéra de Palais Garnier. The 2,700-seat auditorium was supposed to make opera accessible and affordable for all, but the austere design is not really conducive to enjoyment of grand opera, despite the shops and metro exit integrated into the building to reinforce the idea of a "people's opera".

Pages 114–15: walk among the graves at Cimetière du Père Lachaise and you will understand why they say "you haven't lived until you've died in Paris."

Filets de Sole aux Girolles

Fillets of sole with chanterelle mushrooms

It always amazes me that although Paris is so far from the sea, you can find the freshest fish in almost every market and restaurant. In fall, you'll see wild mushrooms alongside the fish; if you can't find saffron-colored chanterelles use any pale-colored wild mushrooms.

SERVES 4
PREPARATION TIME: 10 MINUTES
COOKING TIME: 20 MINUTES

4 large Dover sole fillets, skinned	150g/5oz chanterelle mushrooms
salt and freshly ground white pepper	1tbsp chopped fresh parsley
	pinch of saffron threads
50g/2oz/¼ cup butter	150ml/5fl oz/⅔ cup heavy (double) cream
510ml/18fl oz/2¼ cups fish stock	1 large egg yolk

Preheat the oven to 200°C/400°F/gas mark 6. Halve the sole fillets lengthwise and lay them on a work surface, skinned-side-up. Season and roll up, securing them with a wooden toothpick. Use a little butter to grease a baking dish large enough to take the fillets in one layer. Put in the rolls and pour on the stock. Cover tightly with foil and bake for 10–12 minutes, until the fish is just cooked through.

While the fish is cooking, trim off the woody ends of the mushrooms and wipe the caps with a damp cloth. Halve or quarter any large ones. Heat the remaining butter in a skillet (frying pan) until foaming and sauté the mushrooms for 3–4 minutes, until just tender. Sprinkle with choppedparsley, season with salt and pepper, and keep hot.

Lift the cooked sole fillets on to a warmed serving dish and keep them warm. Strain the cooking liquid into a small saucepan, add the saffron, and boil until the liquid is reduced by half. Stir in the cream, simmer briefly, then turn off the heat.

Lightly beat the egg yolk in a bowl, add a ladleful of the hot sauce, and stir well. Stir the egg mixture into the sauce in the pan and cook very gently for 1–2 minutes, until slightly thickened; do not allow to boil. Season with salt and pepper. Stir the mushrooms into the sauce and pour it over and around the sole fillets.

Petits Pots au Chocolat et à l'Orange

Creamy chocolate and orange mousses

Almost every traditional bistro and brasserie serves a version of these rich little chocolate pots. I like them flavored with orange, which adds an extra appeal, but they are equally delicious plain, or made with coffee instead of the orange juice. Crisp *langue de chat* ("cat's tongue") cookies go brilliantly with the petits pots.

SERVES 4
PREPARATION TIME: 15 MINUTES
COOKING TIME: 10 MINUTES

125g/4½oz/4½ squares best bittersweet chocolate (70 percent cocoa solids)	1 orange
	4 large eggs, separated
	pinch of salt
grated zest and juice of	1tbsp superfine (caster) sugar

Break the chocolate into small pieces and melt it in a large bowl set over a pan of simmering water, or in a microwave oven.

Heat the orange juice to just below boiling, then strain it into the melted chocolate. Stir until very smooth and take the bowl off the simmering water. Beat the egg yolks into the melted chocolate one at a time.

Beat the egg whites with the salt until very stiff. Fold them and the orange zest into the chocolate and add the sugar.

Spoon the mixture into ramekins or espresso cups and refrigerate until firm.

Le Marais, Beaubourg & Ile St-Louis

(3rd & 4th arrondissements)

When you look at the fabulously opulent *hôtels particuliers* (mansions) that grace this fascinating area today, it's hard to believe that such a chic neighborhood emerged from an insalubrious swamp (*marais* means "marsh"). Drained and cleared in the twelfth century by a Christian religious order, the Marais attracted the Jewish community, who populated the cramped area around the rue des Juifs ("street of the Jews") — now called rue Ferdinand-Duval.

Le Marais, Beaubourg & Ile St-Louis
(3rd & 4th arrondissements)

The Marais was not considered to be a Jewish ghetto but rather a *pletzl* (Yiddish for "little plaza"). The tight-knit community lived and worked in the maze of narrow streets until the Middle Ages, when Jews were expelled from France en masse, only returning after the Revolution. The 1960s brought an influx of Sephardi refugees from North Africa, whose exotic cuisine now complements the Central European food of the Ashkenazi community.

The Marais was really put on the map when Charles V relocated the royal court there in the fourteenth century. Three hundred years on, it became *the* place to live when, in 1605, Henry IV laid out the enchanting place Royale (renamed the place des Vosges by Napoleon), with its magnificent mansions for his courtiers or, more likely, the royal mistresses. No doubt he regretted installing his former wife, the infamous Reine Margot, in the turreted Hôtel de Sens (you can still see it at number 1 rue du Figuier), where she led a life of scandal and debauchery among the courtesans, literati, and glitterati who were attracted to the area. Less dubious female residents included literary ladies like Madame de Sévigné, whose gorgeous mansion, with its immaculate courtyard and gardens, now forms part of the Musée Carnavalet.

One of France's most popular kings, Henry IV, whose court also lived in this area, became famous for his compassion, and his love of good food. He declared that "every peasant in my kingdom shall have a *poule au pot* (a chicken in his pot) on Sundays".

The place des Vosges is also the oldest public square in Paris. It's a delight to wander through the elegant arcades with their antique shops, art galleries, and salons de thé, and past the sumptuous seventeenth-century buildings.

By contrast, the charming narrow medieval streets are full of quirky delights. In the heart of the bustling Jewish quarter, black-hatted orthodox men rub shoulders with the flamboyant gay population as they throng through the medley of butchers', bakers', bookshops, and trendy boutiques. The rue des Rosiers and rue des Ecouffes are fragrant with frying onions, falafel, and doner kebab (known here as *shawarma*) sold out of small shop fronts; there's even one selling kosher sushi. The windows of boulangeries and pâtisseries entice you with rye and poppy-seed bread, braided challas, cheesecake, and honeyed pastries, while deli counters bulge with traditional delicacies — golden latkes, gefilte fish, and eggplant (aubergine) caviar. Everything, from corned beef to seedcake, is *cacher* (kosher) and the choice is overwhelming. If you want to taste traditional Jewish food, it's best to go on a Sunday, when all the restaurants and shops are open (they close on Saturdays). Make sure to go hungry, feast your eyes and stomach, and enjoy the extraordinary mixture of elegance, tradition, and eccentric charm that encapsulates this beguiling neighborhood.

There could hardly be a greater contrast with the exuberance of the Marais than the seedy but vibrant Beaubourg area, dominated by its extraordinary love-it-or-hate-it the Centre Pompidou (popularly known simply as "Beaubourg"), the first of Paris's contemporary buildings and certainly one of the most outrageous. Conceived by President Georges Pompidou in 1969 as a way of bringing culture to the man in the street, this bold museum of modern art opened in 1977 to the amazement of some and admiration or horror of others.

These days, we have become used to the concept of "inside-out" buildings, with primary-colored pipes, ducts, and escalators snaking around the outside, but at the time, Richard Rogers' and Enzo Piano's iconic structure was like nothing ever seen before.

Although the "high-tech" style had already become outmoded by the time the building was opened, there was some method in its madness. The brightly colored pipes aren't just a decorative feature; they are color-coded by function — green for water, blue for air-conditioning, and yellow for electricity — — with the bright red escalators completing the quartet of colors. Inside the external steel skeleton, the vast expanse of glass makes the building extraordinarily light.

The Centre Pompidou contains one of the world's largest collections of modern art, from the twentieth century to the present, with works by some of the greatest exponents of the Fauvist, cubist, and surrealist movements.

When you are sated with the bewildering array of the beautiful and the strange, you can take the outside glass elevator to the top floor for a break in the vast, open-air terrace café or the smart, ultra-trendy Georges restaurant, with their panoramic views.

Alternatively, picnic in front of the Stravinsky fountain (opposite) in the place Igor Stravinsky. It has sixteen sculptures (including a pair of pouting lips, a dragon, a hat, a treble clef, an elephant, and a well-endowed woman) that spin and spurt water, representing elements from the composer's ballet *The Rite of Spring*.

Pages 118-19: the colorful Center Pompidou, designed by Richard Rogers.

Shops in Le Marais, Beaubourg & Ile St-Louis

Cacao et Chocolat

A luscious chocolate fountain in the shop window will lure you inside the Marais branch of this Aztec-themed chocolate shop, which overflows with cascades of chocoholic treats. The delectable macaroons, éclairs, truffles, cocoa, and all manner of delicious chocolate confections can be prettily packed or enjoyed at the bar with a cup of real hot chocolate or coffee.

36 RUE VIEILLE DU TEMPLE, 01 42 71 50 06

Food

Claude Deloffre indulges her passion for food and cooking in this colorful art gallery and bookshop. She stocks a huge variety of books in French, English, and Japanese on every culinary subject from viennoiserie to vegetable peelings (honestly!). Unfortunately, she doesn't

serve food or refreshments, but you are welcome to browse for as long as you like, until hunger pangs drive you out in search of sustenance.

58 RUE CHARLOT, 01 42 72 68 97

Izraël

An Aladdin's cave of seasonings and spices from every continent, a plethora of pepper, pimento, and all things aromatic. You'll find sacks of dried beans and pulses, fragrant rice, and flour alongside dried fruit and nuts, jars of rare honey, artisanal jams, pickles, sauces, and Indian and Thai curry pastes. Izraël stocks olives and oils, vine leaves and vinegars, and for those with a sweet tooth, there's Turkish delight, Spanish *turrón* (nougat), crystalized fruit, and many wines and spirits.

30 RUE FRANÇOIS MIRON, 01 42 72 66 23

Korcarz

If you're looking for picnic food, you'll find everything you want here. Owned by Polish Holocaust survivors since 1948, this kosher bakery and salon de thé sells super-sized filled rolls, huge éclairs, home-made poppy-seed cakes, and cheesecake baked in vast pans and served by weight, and typically Central European sweet and savory pastries with evocative names: strudels, *zlabia* (deep-fried doughnuts soaked in syrup), and sachertorte.

29 RUE DES ROSIERS, 01 42 77 39 47

Jo Goldenberg

Jo's Russian parents owned this deli-cum-restaurant before the war. They died in a concentration camp, but their octogenarian sons continue to run the business, which has become a local institution, selling everything from sausages and pastrami to chopped liver and chicken soup to takeout or eat in. The restaurant walls are festooned with photos and paintings of relatives — a place where food, family, and history are inextricably linked.

7 RUE DES ROSIERS, 01 48 87 20 16

Marché des Enfants Rouges

Dating from 1777, this is the oldest covered market in Paris. It takes its curious name from the homeless children who were housed in the mission next door, and were dressed from head to toe in red. The market is small, but has a good range of fruit and vegetables, fish and seafood, meat and general groceries. Try white truffles from the Italian traiteur, roast chicken and golden potatoes from the rôtisseur, steaming fragrant couscous, tagines, and b'stilla from Morocco, and tofu croquettes, sushi, and green tea cake from the Japanese stall. The produce and fish stalls are open only four days

a week (Wednesday and Friday mornings, Saturday morning and evening, and Sunday morning) but a trio of traiteurs (Italian, Moroccan, and Japanese) are there from Tuesday to Sunday, serving great-value freshly cooked food to takeout or eat at the counter.

39 RUE DE BRETAGNE

Palais des Thés

Walking into this emporium is like visiting an exotic land. The boxes and caddies that line the walls contain almost 300 different teas from around the world — rare and scented teas, classic blends — all there for you to smell, taste and buy, plus books about tea, unusual tea sets and stylish accessories.

68 RUE VIELLE DU TEMPLE,
01 48 87 80 60

Sacha Finkelstzajn

You can find almost every kind of Yiddish specialty here, from traditional breads — dark rye, golden braided challas, and chewy bagels — to crisp cheese-and meat-filled boreks, and gefilte fish. Takeout, or buy a coffee and eat on the premises, perched on high stools near the entrance.

27 RUE DES ROSIERS, 01 42 72 78 91

Vert d'Absinthe

It is said that many a nineteenth-century artist and poet succumbed to madness after drinking absinthe, the bitter green spirit made from wormwood. It was banned from sale in 1914, but finally relegitimized in 1988 with a lower alcohol content than the seventy-two percent that plunged Verlaine, Van Gogh, and Baudelaire into insanity. This shop (the only one of its kind in Paris) stocks a dozen or more different absinthes and aniseed liqueurs, including the aptly named Fleurs du Mal, along with pierced spoons, glasses, and carafes that are all part of the ritual of absinthe drinking. There are free tastings and you can buy souvenirs to prove that you survived the experience.

11 RUE D'ORMESSON, 01 42 71 63 73

Mariage Frères

The original shop has been here since 1854 and little seems to have changed. Immaculately white-suited assistants guide you through a voyage of discovery of 550 teas, kept in huge, beautiful canisters. Tea is treated with the same respect as fine wine, and you are encouraged to smell the aroma and feel the quality of the leaves.

There's everything from health-giving green tea with cherry blossom to exceptionally rare Red Robe Chinese tea sold at several hundred euros a kilo, along with original teapots and accessories, tea-flavored jellies, delicious sablés, and even tea-scented candles. Upstairs, there's a small (free) museum with antique caddies, pots, and tea-related paraphernalia. The conservatory-like salon de thé serves afternoon tea, light lunches, and brunch on Sundays, with luscious cakes to accompany your choice of tea.

30 RUE DU BOURG-TIBOURG,
01 42 72 28 11

Restaurants in Le Marais, Beaubourg & Ile St-Louis

L'Ambroisie

The sumptuous seventeenth-century mansion makes the perfect setting for chef Bernard Pacaud's sensational cooking. The 400-year-old stone floor and the gilt and dark wood of the main room are enhanced with fabulous Aubusson tapestries, but the small back room is best avoided. Service is formal, as befits the seriousness of the food, with seasonal and signature dishes like langoustines with light curry sauce layered with crisp sesame thin discs of crisp pastry, *feuillantines*, and foie gras flavored with herbs. Desserts are truly ambrosial, the wine list is magisterial, and the prices soar to the heavens.

9 PLACE DES VOSGES, 01 42 78 51 45

L'As du Fallafel

Photos of film stars and pop idols adorn the walls of this tiny, crowded falafel and *shawarma* (doner kebab) restaurant as testament to its popularity. On Sundays, you will have to queue up either outside for a takeout or inside for a seat in the simple, frenetically buzzy restaurant, but it's worth the wait to enjoy crisp, fresh falafel with fried eggplant (aubergine), flavorful hummus, tahini, and eggplant caviar, or succulent shawarma. The home-made hot sauce is deliciously spicy and the lemonade wonderfully refreshing. It's all very cheap, but delicious, and truly "ace" Sephardi food.

34 RUE DES ROSIERS, 01 48 87 63 60

Café Beaubourg

Take a seat on the terrace opposite the Centre Pompidou, the perfect place to sit with some refreshment and watch the goings-on in the plaza, or push through theatrical red velvet curtains into the Costes brothers' 1980s split-level concrete café-bar-restaurant. Here, black-clad waiters zoom past soaring concrete columns, up and down the stairs, balancing trays laden with classy cocktails and coffees for the trendy (and wealthy) clientèle, who come to be seen as much as to see. The décor seems rather passé, but the food — omelets, seared steak tartare, and pastries — is still excellent, if pricey.

43 RUE ST-MERRI, 01 48 87 63 96

Chez Marianne

Something of an institution, the ever-popular Chez Marianne serves both Central European and North African Jewish food. The two dining rooms (the one at the back is quieter) and summer terrace are always packed and service can be impatient, but take your time to choose a selection of four or six *zakouski* (appetizers), such as chopped liver, outstandingly good hummus, brik, and excellent falafel. Succulent smoked salmon and pastrami are served on rye bread, and the substantial pastries and cheesecake are classics. If you can't face the queue for a table, everything is available to takeout from the deli, including fabulous falafel sandwiches.
2 RUE DES HOSPITALIÈRES,
01 42 72 18 86

Les Enfants Rouges

You'll find that the blackboard menu at this friendly old-fashioned little bistro, right next to the market, offers popular favorites like chicken liver terrine, oysters, and *andouillettes* (chitterlings). For hearty appetites, venison daube and steak are tasty options, and the crème brûlée is sensational. The wine list contains some special vintages.
90 RUE DES ARCHIVES,
01 48 87 80 61

Chez Jenny

Here you'll find a little corner of Alsace in the Marais. The series of rooms that makes up this cavernous brasserie (part of the ubiquitous Flo chain) is decorated with splendid marquetry scenes of Alsace by Charles Spindler. Friendly waitresses serve platters of briny fresh fruits de mer and gargantuan choucroûte piled with sausages and pork. If you've got room, finish your meal with a slice of traditional *gugelhopf* (yeast cake) and wash it all down with a selection of fine Alsace wines.
38 BOULEVARD DU TEMPLE, 01 44 54 39 00

Restaurants in Le Marais, Beaubourg & Ile St-Louis

Georges

The views alone make eating at this ultra-trendy restaurant worthwhile. Perched on the sixth floor of the Centre Pompidou, the outdoor terrace and minimalist space-age restaurant offer stupendous views over Paris. Take the external elevator (if you use the escalators, you'll have to pay the entrance fee) and move heaven and earth to ensure that you get a table beside the vast picture windows for a spectacular vista. The innovative menu offers dishes with an Oriental slant and names to match, like Mandarin crispy duck and a chilli beef dish, *la tigre qui pleut* (the weeping tigress), plus oysters and foie gras *"suffisant pour deux"* (enough for two).

CENTRE POMPIDOU, SIXTH FLOOR, 01 44 78 47 99

Le Pamphlet

The menu changes every day at this most elegant bistro, with well-spaced tables, wood-paneled walls, and a beamed ceiling. Chef Alain Carrière includes plenty of dishes from his native south-west France, but also imports the freshest fish from Brittany, and often combines the two, as in oysters or sea bass with a light foie gras sauce. Service is charming and prices exceptionally low for the quality of the cooking and the interesting selection of wines.

38 RUE DEBELLEYME, 01 42 72 39 24

Bel Canto

If music be the food of love, this is the place to go for a romantic dinner. Order your meal from four young waiting staff dressed in theatrical finery, then watch them down tools and burst into song, for these are no ordinary waiters, but former students of the Paris Conservatoire — a soprano, mezzo, tenor, and baritone — all trained as top-flight opera singers. Throughout the evening, they perform dual roles as waiters and singers, punctuating the flow of classic Italian food with operatic arias and Neapolitan songs. The concept has become so popular that there are now several branches in Paris.

72 QUAI DE L'HÔTEL-DE-VILLE,
01 42 78 30 18

Pitchi Poï

Set in a quiet traffic-free square with a terrace for outdoor dining, the interior of Pitchi Poï is reminiscent of Morocco, with brightly colored cushions and stained-glass candle holders. The menu, however, veers towards Central Europe, with rib-sticking winter warmers like goulash, *tchoulent* (a slow-cooked dish of duck, beans, barley, and potatoes), and osso buco. Lighter offerings include selections of *zakouski* (appetizers), smoked salmon with sour cream and dill, or chopped chicken livers. A range of vodkas completes the picture, but Hungarian and Israeli wines are available too. On Sundays, there's a popular all-you-can-eat buffet.

7 PLACE DU MARCHÉ STE-CATHERINE,
01 42 77 46 15

404

As bustling and crowded as a colorful Berber kasbah, this convivial Algerian restaurant serves some of the best couscous, tagines, and Algerian wines in Paris. Start with a mint cocktail to put you in the party mood, before moving on to a delicious salad of tomatoes, onions and bell peppers, or eggplant (aubergine) and garlic. If you enjoy the combination of sweet and savory, try the pigeon *b'stilla* (a sweet-and-savory pie) followed by fresh fruit salad or one of the deliciously sweet pistachio pastries. There's toe-tapping music at night and an excellent Berber brunch at weekends.

69 RUE DES GRAVILLIERS,
01 42 74 57 81

Artichauts à la Juive

Deep-fried artichokes

Sephardi Jews brought this delicious Italian recipe to Paris when they moved into the Marais area in the 1960s. It is best made when tiny, very tender artichokes are in season. Look for *artichauts violets* (purple artichokes) in the market.

SERVES 6
PREPARATION TIME: 15 MINUTES
COOKING TIME: 15–20 MINUTES

6 very tender artichokes (*artichauts violets* if possible)
juice of 1 lemon
salt and freshly ground black pepper
vegetable or sunflower oil for deep-frying

Snap off the artichoke stems leaving about 2cm/¾ inch. If the outer leaves are tough, pull them off, but otherwise leave the artichokes intact. Pull the leaves apart to see whether there is a hairy choke at the center; if so, scrape it out with a teaspoon. Rub any cut edges with lemon juice to prevent discoloration and sprinkle the artichokes with salt and pepper. Lay them on their sides on the work surface and with the palm of your hand press gently to flatten the artichokes without damaging them.

In a shallow saucepan or deep skillet (frying pan) large enough to hold all the artichokes, heat the oil until hot, then put in the artichokes upside-down. Fry over a medium heat for about 10–15 minutes, turning the artichokes every minute and taking care that they do not over-brown. Push a skewer or knife tip through the stem into the heart; they are done when it slides in easily.

Take the artichokes out of the oil and drain on paper towels. Add a little more oil to the pan and reheat until very hot. Return the artichokes to the pan, upside-down, and fry again, turning frequently, until they are very crisp and golden brown. Drain on fresh paper towels and serve.

Pages 130–1: the glass-and-steel Center Pompidou in Beaubourg district, which opened in 1977.

Falafel

Deep-fried garbanzo bean (chickpea)balls

This is perfect, if messy, picnic food to enjoy in the place des Vosges.

SERVES 4
PREPARATION TIME: 20 MINUTES, PLUS 24 HOURS SOAKING AND 1 HOUR CHILLING
COOKING TIME: 15 MINUTES

200g/7oz/packed 1 cup dried garbanzo beans (chickpeas), soaked for at least 24 hours
1 onion, chopped
2 garlic cloves, chopped
30g/1oz/1½ cups cilantro (coriander), roughly chopped
1tsp cumin seeds
1tsp coriander seeds
½tsp baking powder
salt and freshly ground black pepper

pinch of cayenne
oil, for deep-frying

TO SERVE:
4 Arab or pitta breads
200g/7oz hummus or eggplant (aubergine) "caviar" (see page 137)
1 red bell pepper, seeded and white membrane removed, cut into thin strips
1–2 handfuls of frisée lettuce

To make the falafel, drain the garbanzo beans. Wash them thoroughly in fresh water and blitz them in a food processor until they have the consistency of coarse breadcrumbs. Add the onion, garlic, and cilantro and pulse to a fairly coarse purée, scraping the purée from the sides of the bowl after every few pulses. Transfer the purée to a bowl.

Heat a small skillet (frying pan) over a medium heat and dry-fry the cumin and coriander seeds for a few moments, until they smell very aromatic. Crush them finely in a mortar and stir them into the bean purée along with the baking powder. Season with salt, pepper, and cayenne. Cover and chill in the refrigerator for about 1 hour.

Take walnut-sized pieces of purée and roll them into balls. Heat the oil in a large, deep skillet or saucepan and deep-fry the balls in batches for about 3 minutes, until golden brown. Lift out the falafel with a slotted spoon and drain on paper towels.

If you prefer a hot sandwich, warm the bread and falafel in a hot oven for about 5 minutes. Halve the pittas and open up the pockets. Spread the hummus or "eggplant caviar" over the insides and fill the pockets with the falafel, red bell pepper strips, and lettuce.

Coq au Vin
Chicken in red wine

Coq au vin was originally made using an old rooster, which had outlived its usefulness and benefited from long, slow cooking in a full-bodied red wine to tenderize it. A meaty free-range chicken will, however, produce a wonderfully tender, flavorful dish.

SERVES 6
PREPARATION TIME: 20 MINUTES
COOKING TIME: 1–1½ HOURS

1 large free-range chicken, about 2.5kg/5½lb, cut up
salt and freshly ground black pepper
25g/1oz/2tbsp butter
1tbsp oil
150g/5oz *lardons* or thick-cut bacon, diced
18 baby onions, peeled
275g/10oz button mushrooms
2tbsp Cognac
2 garlic cloves, finely chopped

1 bottle full-bodied red wine (Chambertin for preference)
1 home-made bouquet garni (½ celery stalk, thyme, parsley, and 2 bay leaves tied together)
beurre manié (1½tbsp all-purpose (plain) flour mashed with 2tbsp softened butter)
2–3 tbsp chopped fresh, flat-leaf parsley, to garnish

Season the chicken pieces. In a wide flameproof casserole, heat half the butter with the oil until hot, add the lardons and onions, and fry until lightly browned. Remove them with a slotted spoon and set aside. Add the mushrooms to the casserole, fry briefly, remove, them and add to the bacon and onions.

Heat the rest of the butter in the casserole, put in the chicken pieces and fry until lightly golden all over. Sprinkle in the Cognac and flame it. When the flames die down, add the garlic and wine and bring to a boil. Add the bouquet garni, cover, and simmer very gently for 30 minutes. Gently stir in the bacon, onions, and mushrooms, cover and continue to cook for another 30–60 minutes, until the chicken is tender and almost falling off the bone.

Use a slotted spoon to lift the chicken, bacon, onions and mushrooms on to a warmed serving platter. Discard the bouquet garni. Bring the cooking juices to just below boiling point and whisk in the beurre manié. Simmer for 3–4 minutes until the sauce is thick and shiny. Taste and season accordingly, then pour it over the chicken and vegetables. Garnish with parsley and serve.

Rognons de Veau à la Moutarde
Veal kidneys in mustard sauce

This is a classic bistro or brasserie dish that I love. The combination of tender kidneys and creamy mustard sauce is superb. Be careful not to overcook the kidneys or they will become tough. Serve them with plain boiled potatoes, and some lightly steamed spinach.

SERVES 4
PREPARATION TIME: 10 MINUTES
COOKING TIME: 10 MINUTES

1tbsp olive oil
salt and freshly ground black pepper
500g/1lb 2oz veal kidneys, halved lengthwise
1tbsp butter

2 shallots, finely chopped
2tbsp Cognac
150ml/5fl oz/⅔ cup heavy (double) cream
1–1½tbsp Dijon mustard

Heat the olive oil in a deep skillet (frying pan) until it begins to smoke. Season the kidneys with salt and pepper, put them in the pan, and sauté for about 4 minutes until lightly colored all over. They should still be pink in the middle. Lift them out with a slotted spoon and set aside to drain on paper towels.

Melt the butter in the same pan and gently sweat the shallots for about 3 minutes, until soft but not colored. Turn the heat up high, pour in the Cognac, and simmer until the liquid is reduced by half.

Mix the cream with as much mustard as you wish, pour it into the pan, add the kidneys, and reheat them over a low heat, stirring to coat them with the sauce. Serve at once.

Landmarks

It would be difficult to find two more contrasting areas: the ancient maze-like le Marais with its elegant mansions, museums, smart bistros and fashion boutiques, and chic residents and Beaubourg with its hordes of visitors and decidedly carnival atmosphere. However, it is easy to see why Beaubourg is one of Paris's most popular attractions, not just for the architecturally outrageous Centre Pompidou, one of the world's most famous modern art galleries, but also for the lively atmosphere of the plaza in front of it. Visitors throng the sloping space, watching performance artists of every kind — mime artists, jugglers, fire-eaters, and unicyclists — put on a non-stop show.

Musée Carnavalet

You can trace the whole history of Paris in this enormous museum, housed in two adjoining mansions, the sixteenth-century Hôtel Carnavalet (home of Madame de Sévigné) and the seventeenth-century Hôtel le Peletier, with a glorious courtyard in front. It's all there, from prehistoric times to the present day. Sculptures, paintings, memorabilia, and sumptuous recreations of rooms, each furnished in the style of a different period, evoke the spirit of Paris past. Highlights include the unbelievably opulent Grand Salon de l'Hôtel de Uzès, two rooms dedicated to Madame de Sévigné, and Napoleon's 110-piece picnic case. There's a recreation of Marcel Proust's study, cork-lined to exclude any noise, where he spent his last reclusive years, eating nothing all day.

Musée Picasso

Tucked away in rue Thorigny, the beautifully restored seventeenth-century Hôtel Salé, with its spectacularly opulent interior, houses the world's largest collection of works by Pablo Picasso. Cross the cobbled courtyard to enter a world of pink and blue periods, modernism and cubism. Paintings, sculptures, drawings, prints, and collages from his precocious childhood up to his death are displayed, as well as a personal collection of works by the artists he admired: Cézanne, Degas, Braque, and Matisse. Picasso's own works, arranged chronologically, take you on a fascinating journey through his entire eighty-year career. The lovely garden makes a wonderful setting for Picasso's ground-breaking cubist sculptures. From April through October, enjoy the scene over a cup of tea in the garden café.

Place des Vosges

For gastronomes, the main attraction of Paris's oldest square (which dates from 1612) is number 9, home to the three-Michelin-starred Ambroisie, one of the most luxurious restaurants in France. If dining there can only be a dream, at least you can appreciate the elegance of the thirty-six hôtels particuliers that surround the square, nine on each side, with their distinctive red-brick and stone facades and steeply pitched gray-slate roofs. Shop in the rue des Rosiers for provisions, then come back and sit by a fountain to eat as you admire the trees, immaculate gravel paths, ornate lampposts, and the statue of Louis XIII. You'll notice that the middle houses on the north and south sides of the square are larger than the rest. These were the royal pavilions, the Pavillon du Roi and the Pavillon de la Reine which is now a luxurious small hotel with a gorgeous courtyard garden. Lesser mortals who have been lucky (and rich) enough to live in the square include Cardinal Richelieu, writers Alphonse Daudet and Victor Hugo (who lived at number 6), and, more recently, the painter Francis Bacon and the architect Richard Rogers.

Musée d'Art et d'Histoire du Judaïsme

Housed in the restored seventeenth-century Hôtel de St-Aignan, a refuge for Jewish immigrants from eastern Europe in the nineteenth century, the museum relates a poignant history. The residents were arrested in World War II and sent to concentration camps. The tragic event is commemorated in Christian Boltanski's installation, *Les Habitants de l'Hôtel de St-Aignan en 1939*.

The museum creates a vivid evocation of Jewish life and culture from the Middle Ages to the present day, focusing mainly on French Jews. Some of the highlights include treasures from Paris synagogues, like a rare menorah dating from before the expulsion of the Jews in the fourteenth century, and a gorgeously painted eighteenth-century *ketubah* (marriage contract). You can study the fascinating archives of the infamous Dreyfus affair, and there are fine works by the acclaimed Jewish artists Marc Chagall and Amadeo Modigliani.

Mont Blanc

Meringue nests with chestnut purée and cream

This wonderfully indulgent pudding was created in Chamonix in honor of Mont Blanc, but was soon adopted by Parisian chefs. It is best made with fresh chestnuts, but works very well with unsweetened chestnut purée (the sweetened variety is too sugary).

SERVES 8–10

PREPARATION TIME: 10 MINUTES (LONGER IF YOU USE
  FRESH CHESTNUTS)

COOKING TIME: ABOUT 2 HOURS FOR THE MERINGUE BASES

1.35kg/3lb fresh chestnuts,
  peeled and skinned, or 2 x
  435g/15½oz cans of
  unsweetened chestnut purée
1 vanilla bean (pod), split
  lengthwise (if using fresh
  chestnuts)
50g/2oz/⅓ cup superfine
  (caster) sugar
110ml/4fl oz/½ cup heavy
  (whipping) cream
1–2tbs confectioners' (icing)
  sugar

MERINGUE:
4 large egg whites
pinch of salt
225g/8oz/packed 1 cup
  superfine (caster) sugar
½tsp vanilla extract

Preheat the oven to 120°C/250°F/gas mark ½. Line two baking sheets with baking parchment and mark out eight to ten 9-cm/3-inch circles.

To make the meringue, use a scrupulously clean, dry bowl, whisk the egg whites with the salt until they form soft peaks. Use a large spoon gently to fold in half the sugar, and then add the vanilla extract and the rest of the sugar, a tablespoon at a time, beating until the whites are firm enough to stay in the bowl when you turn it upside-down. Spread or pipe the meringue inside the marked circles. Cook the meringue bases in the oven for about 2 hours, until dry but not colored.

If you are using fresh chestnuts, put them in a saucepan with the vanilla bean, cover with water, and bring to a boil. Cover the pan and simmer for 25–30 minutes, until the chestnuts are very tender. Remove the vanilla, drain the chestnuts and purée them.

Using a small, heavy-bottomed pan, boil the superfine sugar and 50ml/2fl oz/¼ cup water to make a light syrup and leave to cool. Fold enough syrup into the chestnut purée to thin it for piping, but leave it thick enough to hold its shape. Put it into a pastry bag with a 4-mm/⅙-inch (no.0) tip and pipe it in a spiral on to the meringue bases, mounding it up in the center.

Whip the cream with the confectioners' sugar until stiff and pipe it on top of the chestnut purée, piling it high in the middle like a mini Mont Blanc.

Caviar d'Aubergines

Eggplant (aubergine) "caviar"

The best "poor man's caviar" I ate in the Marais was at Chez Marianne, where it starred in the array of appetizers. It is very easy to make at home, so buy some fat, shiny, purple eggplants (aubergines) in the market (don't use the round-white-striped variety for this dish) and give it a try?

SERVES 4–6
PREPARATION TIME: 10 MINUTES
COOKING TIME: ABOUT 30–40 MINUTES

2 eggplants (aubergines)
2–3 tbsp olive oil
2 garlic cloves, peeled
    and crushed with a little
    coarse sea salt

juice of 1 lemon
salt and freshly ground
    black pepper

Preheat the oven to 220°C/425°F/gas mark 7 or the broiler (grill) to high. Lightly rub a little oil over the eggplants, put them on a baking tray and cook in the oven for 30–40 minutes until very soft, or keep turning them under the broiler (grill) until the skin blisters and the flesh is soft. The latter method takes less time but is more labor-intensive.

As soon as the eggplants are cool enough to handle, scoop out the flesh, put it in a food processor or blender with the garlic, remaining olive oil, and lemon juice to taste, and blitz.

I prefer a coarser texture, but you may like it to be smooth. Just stop when it reaches the consistency you like best.

Season with salt and pepper, stir, and cover tightly with plastic wrap until ready to use. Serve with black olives and warmed pitta bread cut into strips.

Pages 138–9: the sumptuous place des Vosges, completed in 1612, with its superb formal public garden.

La Tour Eiffel, Ecole Militaire & Les Invalides

(7th arrondissement)

If you had to choose a single image to capture the magic of Paris, it would surely be the Eiffel Tower, which still dominates the city more than one hundred years after it was built. From the top, the view on a clear day is unforgettable, like viewing the city from a light aircraft. And what a view!

La Tour Eiffel, Ecole Militaire & Les Invalides
(7th arrondissement)

Immediately below the Eiffel Tower stretches the Champ-de-Mars (field of Mars, the god of war), where the Romans fought the Parisii tribe in 52 BC. Once this was an area of vineyards and market gardens — the ultimate farmers' market, where fresh produce was sold to the public direct from the fields.

In the eighteenth century, the imposing Ecole Militaire (Military Academy) was built at the southern end, and the Champ-de-Mars was laid out to become the training ground for soldiers. Among the recruits was Napoleon Bonaparte, who enrolled at the tender age of fifteen and left as a sub-lieutenant in 1785 with a graduation report noting that he "would go very far in the right circumstances". As a drill ground, of course, the area was no longer used for farming, but potatoes were still grown in the ditches that were dug around the perimeter.

In 1791, the Champ-de-Mars was the scene of one of the bloodiest massacres of the Revolution. Troops fired on the crowd who had gathered to demand the removal of Louis XVI, killing over fifty citizens.

Today, the field could hardly be less militaristic. It's a beautifully manicured public park, where old men play boules, fashionistas walk their dogs on its geometric paths, office workers and tourists picnic and sunbathe in fine weather on the grass, and carefree children play or ride the painted horses on the old-fashioned carousel.

On a sunny day, the most striking feature visible from the Eiffel Tower is the golden dome of the Eglise du Dôme, part of the Hôtel des Invalides complex, built by the Sun King, Louis XIV (never one to hide his light under a bushel), to symbolize his own celestial glory. The chapels are filled with the tombs of

France's great generals, with Napoleon's massive mausoleum as the centerpiece.

The streets behind les Invalides may be less stellar from a military point of view, but they are a paradise for food lovers. From chocolate to caviar, you'll find the finest that Paris can offer. Walk just two blocks west and you'll come to the pedestrianized rue Clerc. It's a joy to stroll down this charming, cobbled street where you'll discover a little bit of food heaven. Whether you want to eat out or buy food to cook at home, you'll find it here. It's hard not to be tempted by the alluring window displays of hand-cured charcuterie, seductive chocolates, rare olive oils or honeys, and irresistible breads and pastries. Sidewalk tables are perfect for people-watching with an aperitif, and those outside the world-famous traiteurs Lenôtre and Davoli, the latter probably the best Italian delicatessen in Paris, are always packed with bons viveurs enjoying coffee and cakes, or inventive salads.

As if all this weren't enough, the twice-weekly Saxe-Breteuil market is one of the most attractive in Paris. Under the shadow of the Eiffel Tower, you can feast your eyes on the freshest, newest seasonal produce before buying the perfect picnic to enjoy on the lawns of the Champ-de-Mars.

It's easy to understand why this chic neighborhood sustains so many high-quality food shops and restaurants. The proximity of the Seine, the quiet elegance of the streets, and even the Eiffel Tower itself make this area one of the pleasant, most sophisticated places to live in Paris, despite the invasion of the six million tourists who visit the tower every year.

Pages 140–1: a view of the matrix of iron beams from directly beneath the Eiffel Tower.

Shops in La Tour Eiffel, Ecole Militaire & Les Invalides

Grégory Renard
The melt-in-the mouth macaroons may well be the best in Paris. Once you've had one, the temptation to try all fourteen flavors — from chocolate and bitter orange to nougat or apple and cinnamon, and the combination of chocolate with flakes of fleur de sel — is irresistible. Hand-made confectionery includes amusing chocolate and marzipan animals.
120 RUE ST-DOMINIQUE, 01 47 05 19 17

Jean-Paul Hévin
A chocolate Jimmy Choo shoe lures you into this architect-designed branch of Hévin's chocolate heaven, with its gorgeous display of sticky marrons glacés, macaroons, fruit jellies, and gloriously rich cakes alongside the rightly famous selection of beautifully crafted and innovative chocolates. For a witty gift, there are always the tins of chocolate "caviar", or "woven" chocolate hearts in purple-lined boxes for romantics.
16 AVENUE DE LA MOTTE-PIQUET, 01 45 51 77 48

Epicerie Fine
The aromas of coffee and tea are irresistible as you enter Pascal Mièvre's little grocery, where everything he sells is of the highest quality. Jars of exotic spices and crystalized ginger transport you to Morocco, and there's a fine selection of teas, jams, and chutneys.
8 RUE DU CHAMP-DE-MARS, 01 47 05 98 18

Le Fleuriste du Chocolat
Thierry Bonnet's tiny shop is a riot of colorful floristry, from individual pot plants to brilliant bouquets and floral arrangements. But sniff the petals and you won't smell flowers, because every plant and flower is made of chocolate with a brightly painted crisp sugar coating. The artistry is astonishing; it all looks too good to eat, but eat it you can — if you can bear to destroy such things of beauty.
49 AVENUE DE LA BOURDONNAIS, 01 45 56 13 04

Lenôtre

On one side of this branch of the famous traiteur you'll find a selection of jaw-droppingly beautiful cakes and fruit tarts, along with mouthwatering chocolates and mounds of macaroons in myriad flavors. Lenôtre makes some of the best macaroons in Paris; you can even buy them painted on teatime china. The other side is devoted to takeout prepared dishes — ideal for a smart picnic. Choose from an array of succulent salmon coulibiac, quiches, and appetizing salads, take home a microwaveable meal of duckling with foie gras and creamy polenta, or pick up something from the cheese counter.
36 AVENUE DE LA MOTTE-PIQUET,
01 45 55 71 25

Marie-Anne Cantin

Marie-Anne inherited her passion for cheese from her father Christian, himself a maître-fromager. She is probably the most famous and well-respected affineuse de fromages in Paris, and justifiably so because she's the official supplier of cheese to the Elysée Palace. In the seven cellars below her shop, she matures up to 150 fabulous cheeses, mostly unpasteurized, including forty or fifty goat varieties, lovingly nurturing them to perfection. If you find the vast choice bewildering, Marie-Anne or her husband, Antoine Dias, will gladly give expert advice on the perfect cheese for you.
12 RUE DU CHAMP-DE-MARS,
01 45 50 43 94

Marché Saxe-Breteuil

One of Paris's oldest and most attractive *marchés volants* (roving markets), this is also among the most popular. The large market, open Thursday and Saturday mornings and always bustling with life, stretches along the avenue de Saxe, under the shadow of the Eiffel Tower. Beneath their striped awnings, the lines of stalls are laden with artistic arrangements of the finest and freshest seasonal fruit and vegetables — fat white asparagus in summer, crisp juicy apples in the fall. Artisan cheeses, honeys, olive oils, hand-crafted breads, and tarts all vie for attention. Look out for Jacky Lorenzo's justly famous fish and shellfish, and the charcutier Michel Feltin, who uses only locally reared pork for his exceptional products. Go early before the market becomes too crowded.
AVENUE DE SAXE

Shops in La Tour Eiffel, Ecole Militaire & Les Invalides

Michel Chaudun

"Le bon chocolat est celui qui nous procure un choc" ("good chocolate is like an electric shock"), says maître-chocolatier Michel Chaudun, whose hand-made chocolates are truly astounding. His tiny corner shop is a shrine to chocolate; everything from a sculpted Statue of Liberty and Aztec masks to immaculately crafted miniature Hermès purses (handbags) is made from his unique blend of chocolate from nine separate sources. The selection of almost forty different creations includes tiny squares of to-die-for rich truffles in more than a dozen flavors, and an intensely dark, crunchy chocolate filled with an explosion of toasted, crushed cocoa beans. The elegant cream-and-chocolate-ribboned boxes look almost good enough to eat.

149 RUE DE L'UNIVERSITÉ,
01 47 53 74 40

Le Moulin de la Vierge

Basile Kamir is one of Paris's most passionate artisanal bakers. Like his other two boulangeries, this branch is housed in a turn-of-the-twentieth-century bakery, and has a special charm. Traditionally made sourdough bread is a specialty, or try the olive and anchovy fougasse, and the hand-crafted baguettes and round *boules* (loaves).

166 AVENUE DE SUFFREN,
01 47 83 45 55

Pain d'Epis

Thierry Dubois is intensely proud of the artisan breads he bakes, which have been voted the best in Paris. His favorites, the organic mixed-grain *grainetier au levain* and multi-grain *baguette gamme royale*, are available every day, but other loaves feature only on certain days — sunflower-seed *boule aux épices* scented with cinnamon, nutmeg, and cloves is on Tuesdays and Thursdays; *figuier* with figs and spelt, on Mondays, Wednesdays and Fridays. You can buy pavé with green olives on Tuesdays, but you'll have to wait until Wednesday for *le châtaignier*, made with pieces of chestnut. A useful leaflet suggests which breads go with what food. For a picnic, try the generously filled sandwiches, chorizo fougasse, or individual quiches filled with Belgian endive and bacon.

63 AVENUE BOSQUET, 01 45 51 75 01

Secco

The delivery van outside this tiny shop with its flower-painted tiles and romantic ceiling still bears the name Poujauran, but the famous bakery is now called Secco. It remains as popular as ever, with local residents happy to queue for their breakfast fare of feather-light croissants and buttery sablés aux raisins. Delicious baguettes and little square loaves are lavishly filled for lunchtime sandwiches, and well-heeled customers can buy *nouettes*, small muffins made with coarse salt and olive oil to be eaten with caviar.

20 RUE JEAN NICOT, 01 43 17 35 20

Petrossian

Founded by a Russian émigré in 1920, this original emporium represents the ultimate in gastronomic luxury. Displayed on the long wooden counter are beautifully decorated tins of the world's finest caviars from Iran and Kazakhstan and whole foie gras layered with black truffles. Even if you can't afford to buy, it's a fascinating glimpse into the gastronomic world of the super-rich. For those who don't fall into that category, more affordable offerings include smoked salmon and eel, pickled herrings, and smoked cod's roe. Upstairs there's a restaurant; downstairs, you can have caviar with blinis, toast, and sour cream, with a glass of Champagne or vodka. Fifty grams of Imperial Gourmet will cost you dearly, but it will be the most delicious extravagance.

18 BOULEVARD DE LATOUR MAUBOURG, 01 44 11 32 22

Restaurants in La Tour Eiffel, Ecole Militaire & Les Invalides

L'Affriolé

The name of this intimate bistro means "tempted", and that's what you'll be when offered creative seasonal dishes like smoked salmon cannelloni with vegetable tartare, Limousin veal, or braised ox cheek with smoked potato purée. The restaurant is run by young chefs and is popular with trendy young Parisians. The menu changes constantly, so there's always something new to enjoy, and it's a novelty to be served all the dishes at the same time. Lots of little extras are included, from crunchy radishes to home-made candied orange peel and walnuts, and an assortment of creamy petits pots arrives with your coffee. Mosaic tables and faux marble and leather banquettes add to the cozy atmosphere.

17 RUE MALAR, 01 44 18 31 33

Altitude 95

If you need a rest or can't face the ascent to the top of the Eiffel Tower or just want a crafty way to bypass the queues of people for the lift — do your best to secure a window seat at this first-floor restaurant in the north pillar. The décor of nuts and bolts may make you feel you're sitting in an Erector (Meccano) set and the food doesn't always match the views, but it's more than adequate, with osso buco, beef fillet with Bercy sauce, and rabbit terrine to devour while enjoying the outstanding location.

TOUR EIFFEL, NORTH PILLAR, FIRST FLOOR, 01 45 55 20 04

L'Atelier de Joël Robuchon

It's worth the inevitable queueing for a taste of the great Robuchon's inspired cooking at reasonable prices. Reservations are taken only for sittings at 11.30am or 6.30pm. At other times, you'll have to wait before you can perch on a stool at the counter in one of the two bars in the minimalist black-and-red-lacquered dining room, and watch the chefs on the central cooking station prepare exquisite tapas-style first courses and haute cuisine dishes like herb-crusted cod or *volaille de Bresse* (Bresse chicken) stuffed with foie gras. Practically everything is cooked to order; you can watch your fruity soufflé rise before your very eyes. There's a good choice of wines by the glass, including some grands crus.

5 RUE DE MONTALEMBERT, 01 42 22 56 56

Le Divellec

With its splendid location overlooking the esplanade des Invalides, Le Divellec's nautical décor indicates that this is one of Paris's most venerable fish restaurants — hardly surprising when you know that the patron and virtuoso chef, Jacques Le Divellec, is a hearty, blue-eyed Breton with an enduring love of the sea and its inhabitants. Sauces are kept simple, allowing the superbly fresh seafood to speak for itself. The service is formal and the prices sky-high, but you'll find that everything is of the highest quality. An old fashioned dessert trolley groans with deliciously creamy mousses, rum babas, and delectable gâteau St-Honoré.

107 RUE DE L'UNIVERSITÉ, 01 45 51 91 96

Escalope de Saumon à la Crème d'Oseille
Salmon escalopes in creamy sorrel sauce

I order this simple dish whenever I see it on a brasserie menu. The sharpness of the sorrel makes a superb contrast to the richness of the cream and salmon.

SERVES 4
PREPARATION TIME: 5 MINUTES
COOKING TIME: 8–10 MINUTES

4 salmon fillets, about 175g/6oz each, skinned
salt and freshly ground white pepper
150g/5oz young sorrel leaves
120ml/4fl oz/½ cup crème fraîche or heavy (double) cream
50g/2oz/¼ cup unsalted butter

Slice each salmon fillet on the diagonal into three or four thin escalopes and season lightly on both sides with salt and pepper.

Bring a saucepan of water to a boil, drop in the sorrel, and blanch for 1 minute, then drain thoroughly and chop finely.

Put the crème fraîche or heavy cream into a small saucepan with half the butter and the sorrel. Stir and season to taste, being generous with the pepper. Heat gently, stirring with a wooden spoon, until the sauce has thickened enough to coat the back of the spoon. Keep the sauce warm.

Heat the remaining butter in a large skillet (frying pan) until foaming. Put in the salmon escalopes (you may have to cook them in two batches) and cook over a medium-high heat for 1–2 minutes on each side.

Spoon some of the hot sauce on to warm plates and arrange the salmon on top. Serve the rest of the sauce separately.

Petits pois à la Française
Peas with baby onions and lettuce

This classic French dish adds a new dimension to the humble pea. If fresh peas are in season, so much the better, but frozen petits pois work almost as well. Diced ham is often added to make a popular family supper dish.

SERVES 4–6
PREPARATION TIME: 10 MINUTES
COOKING TIME: 30 MINUTES

700g/1½lb shelled fresh peas or frozen petits pois
25g/1oz/2 tbsp butter
2 tsp sugar
1 small romaine lettuce or 2 Bostons (Little Gems), coarsely shredded
12 baby onions, peeled
4 sprigs of fresh chervil
150ml/5fl oz/⅔ cup vegetable stock or water
salt and freshly ground black pepper

Put the peas, half the butter, sugar, lettuce, onions and the chervil in a medium-sized saucepan. Add the stock or water and bring to a boil, then lower the heat. For fresh peas, simmer gently for about 30 minutes until the liquid has reduced to only about 2 tablespoons; frozen peas will need only about 15 minutes. Remove the chervil, stir in the remaining butter, and season to taste.

Restaurants in La Tour Eiffel, Ecole Militaire & Les Invalides

Les Fables de la Fontaine

The simple rustic brick décor of this tiny fish restaurant belies the chef's sophisticated treatments of fresh fish and seafood. The blackboard menu changes according to the market, but often includes bouillabaisse à la façon des Fables de la Fontaine, beautifully presented whole sea bass grilled à la plancha, and scallops baked in the shell with sea-salted butter. Finish with a delectable wedge of vanilla-filled Paris-Brest. This immensely popular restaurant can get very crowded, but if the weather's fine, you can eat in the delightful outdoor courtyard with a fountain.

131 RUE ST-DOMINIQUE, 01 44 18 37 55

Léo le Lion

From outside, the dark wooden window frames and lace curtains give the impression of an archetypal Parisian bistro. The interior is more elegant, with claret-colored walls and cream tablecloths, and the cooking lives up to the surroundings. Chef-patron Didier Méry cooked at Le Divellec for over twenty years and his love of seafood is reflected in the blackboard menus, which also feature seasonal game. Roast king prawns with mushroom or basil risotto is a specialty, and grilled saddle of lamb is a treat. Finish with a honey crème brûlée or pear and red currant sorbet with warm crème anglaise. Service is charming, with Didier's wife Françoise contributing to the relaxed and friendly atmosphere.

23 RUE DUVIVIER, 01 45 51 41 77

Le Chammaré

Brown-suede banquettes, velvet cushions, colorful glass lights, and multicolored glass fish give a relaxed feel to this excellent hybrid restaurant. All the basic ingredients are European (there's even grouse from Scotland in season), but each is enhanced with elements of Mauritian cuisine with an emphasis on exotic fruits and subtle spices. Lobster, king prawns (prawns), and octopus all benefit from the South Sea island touch, and the signature dish of suckling pig cooked like crispy Chinese duck is a delight. If you're feeling adventurous, go for the carte blanche menu, a succession of surprise dishes served with great charm. Desserts might be a refreshing peach sorbet or a rum-soaked savarin.

13 BOULEVARD DE LATOUR MAUBOURG, 01 47 05 50 18

Pegoty's

If you're partial to a full cooked breakfast, or muffins and crumpets seem more attractive than a baguette, you'll find everything you crave at this delightful salon de thé. The décor has an Oriental touch, but breakfast (complete with sausages and fried bread) and afternoon tea, with dainty sandwiches and scones, couldn't be more British. It's a joy to watch elegantly coiffed Parisian ladies of a certain age tucking into eggs and bacon with gusto. Light lunches are also served, and there's a Champagne brunch on Sundays.

79 AVENUE BOSQUET, 01 45 55 84 50

Thoumieux

Run by the same family since it opened in 1923, and still virtually unchanged, this large, elegant establishment just behind Les Invalides is the epitome of a classic 1930s brasserie, with red-plush banquettes, mirrors, and formal, black-jacketed waiters. The family's culinary roots are in the Corrèze region of south-west France and this is reflected in the number of duck-based dishes on offer. You'll notice that meat features large on the menu — the restaurant specialty is Limousin veal and beef — but you'll find almost any classic bistro dish you can imagine, from pig's feet and tête de veau to coq au vin and gargantuan portions of cassoulet. Try to leave room for the excellent home-made grandmère-style desserts.

79 RUE ST-DOMINIQUE, 01 47 05 49 75

Le Violon d'Ingres

You could make a case for renaming this street "rue Christian Constant". The former executive chef of the Hôtel de Crillon (nothing to do with the renowned chocolatier) now owns three eating places on the same block. There's the fishy Fables de la Fontaine, the casual Café Constant, and his original Violon d'Ingres, named after the artist from the chef's home town, Montauban, whose paintings adorn the wall. The cooking is highly accomplished and the ambience chic yet comfortable, but the service can be less than impeccable. More classic than innovative, the menu offers dishes that reflect the season — polenta with truffles, perfectly cooked scallops, and wood pigeon. Dessert, if you have room, might include red fruits in honey and lime with mascarpone.

135 RUE ST-DOMINIQUE, 01 45 55 15 05

Jules Verne

The stupendous view doesn't come cheap at this top-of-the world restaurant, where tables are among the most sought after in Paris. The sombre metallic-and-black décor looks a little dated, but the food has a modern feel, with steamed scallop ravioli with langoustine butter, gamy terrine with foie gras, and fillet of John Dory with garlicky eggplant (aubergine). Desserts are delicious: try the honey and orange blossom ice cream with lacy sesame tuiles, or an intense dark-chocolate mousse layered with *pain d'épices* (spiced gingerbread). It's essential to book well in advance, especially for the evening or if you want a window table.

TOUR EIFFEL, SOUTH PILLAR, SECOND FLOOR, 01 45 55 61 44

Coquilles St-Jacques à la Parisienne

Parisian-style scallops with mushrooms and mashed potato

This classic dish sums up all the sophistication of Parisian seafood cooking. Smile nicely at the fishmonger and he might even be persuaded to clean the scallops for you.

SERVES 4

PREPARATION TIME: 20 MINUTES

COOKING TIME: 1 HOUR 20 MINUTES

2 medium baking potatoes

12 large sea scallops in their shells

200g/7oz/2¼ cups white button mushrooms, thinly sliced

1 tbsp lemon juice

400ml/14fl oz/1¾ cups fish stock

2 large egg yolks

25g/1oz/2tbsp butter

1 tbsp fine breadcrumbs

1 tbsp finely grated Gruyère cheese

SAUCE:

50g/2oz/¼ cup butter

25g/1oz/¼ cup all-purpose (plain) flour

2 large egg yolks

150ml/5fl oz/⅔ cup heavy (double) cream

salt and freshly ground white pepper

Preheat the oven to 240°C/ 475°F/gas mark 9. Put the potatoes into the oven and bake for about 1 hour until very soft.

Meanwhile, prepare the scallops. If they have not been opened and cleaned, scrub the shells under cold water and place in the hot oven for a minute or two, until they open slightly. Slide a strong, flexible knife blade between the flat shell and the scallop and lift off the shell. Thoroughly rinse and dry four of the concave shells and keep them for serving. Pull off any membrane from the scallops, separate the whites from the orange corals, rinse both well, and pat dry. Put them in a saucepan with the mushrooms, lemon juice, and fish stock and gently bring to just below boiling point. Simmer for 1 minute, turn off the heat, and leave the scallops and mushrooms in the stock.

Next make the sauce. Melt the butter, stir in the flour, and cook for 2 minutes. Strain in the stock from the scallops, stirring continuously until smooth. Simmer the sauce for about 15 minutes, whisking occasionally. Mix the egg yolks with the cream in a bowl, add a ladleful of sauce, whisk, and pour the mixture into the saucepan. Simmer until thickened but not boiling, season, and keep warm over a low heat.

When the potatoes are cooked, halve them, scoop out the flesh, and mash it with the remaining two egg yolks and the remaining butter until very smooth. Season to taste and spoon into a pastry (piping) bag with a large fluted tip. Leave the oven on.

Cut each white scallop into three or four slices. Make a layer of mushrooms in each reserved scallop shell, put a coral in each, and then add the sliced scallops. Coat generously with sauce and sprinkle the tops with a mixture of breadcrumbs and Gruyère. Pipe a ribbon of potato around the edge of the shells. Place the scallops on a baking tray in the oven for 3–4 minutes, until bubbling and lightly browned.

Gratin Dauphinoise

Potatoes baked in cream

This irresistibly rich and creamy potato dish is good enough to serve on its own, especially if you layer the potatoes with a sprinkling of grated Comté or Parmesan cheese. It is essential to the creamy texture that the potatoes are cooked through; the thinner you slice them, the less time this will take, but heating the cream also helps to speed things up.

SERVES 6

PREPARATION TIME: 20 MINUTES

COOKING TIME: ABOUT 1¼ HOURS

1kg/2¼lb waxy potatoes

25g/1oz/2tbsp butter, softened

570ml/1 pint/2½ cups light (single) cream

salt and freshly ground black pepper

1 large garlic clove, crushed and finely chopped

Few sprigs of thyme or rosemary (optional)

Preheat the oven to 180°C/350°F/gas mark 4. Peel the potatoes and slice them thinly using a mandoline or food processor. Use some of the butter to grease a shallow ovenproof dish large enough to hold the potatoes in four layers.

Heat the cream to just below boiling point. Make a layer of potatoes in the dish, season, and scatter on a touch of garlic. Pour on a little cream. Make three more layers (or more if you have some potatoes left) in the same way, and then pour on enough cream to cover the top layer of potatoes. Dot the top with the remaining butter, and a few sprigs or thyme or rosemary if you like, cover tightly with foil, and bake for 1 hour.

Increase the oven temperature to 200°C/400°F/gas mark 6. Take off the foil and cook the potatoes for another 15 minutes or so, until they are very tender (test by inserting the tip of a knife), almost all the cream has been absorbed, and the top of the gratin is bubbling and golden.

Landmarks

The 7th arrondissement, which includes the area around the Eiffel Tower, Ecole Militaire and Les Invalides, has more pâtisseries, and probably more tourists per square inch than anywhere else in Paris. Well-heeled residents are catered to by some of the finest restaurants and shops that Paris has to offer. It is a haven for gourmets and fashionistas alike, but its foreign embassies, government ministries, imposing monuments, and broad avenues mean that no trip to Paris would be complete without a visit to some of its famous landmarks. The pièce de résistance is the Eiffel Tower, which was conceived as the high point of the Centennial Exhibition in 1889.

Ecole Militaire

The colonnaded and domed Military Academy dominates the southern end of the Champ-de-Mars and is appropriately impressive. It was commissioned in 1751 by Louis XV and his mistress Madame de Pompadour to train impoverished young gentlemen as soldiers, and designed by Jacques-Ange Gabriel, who laid out the place de la Concorde and the Petit Trianon at Versailles. The two side wings were added to the central pavilion during the Second Empire. The Academy is still in use, and you can look through the imposing gates to watch the recruits going through their paces in the Cour d'Honneur.

Eiffel Tower

It is difficult to imagine that the celebrated and iconic Eiffel Tower, now universally loved, was at first popularly considered a functionless monstrosity. Local residents feared that the 986-foot-high tower would topple over, crushing their homes under its 7,700-ton weight, while 300 leading figures from the arts world petitioned against it "in the name of French taste and endangered French art and history". These days it is one of the world's most visited attractions, with six million tourists a year lining up to ascend the tower to marvel at the forty-six-mile view (at its best one hour before sunset). At night, the filigreed iron girders are illuminated with a golden glow, and since the millennium celebrations there's an added unmissable spectacle. For ten minutes every hour from dusk to 2am, 20,000 bulbs flash and fizz, causing the tower to sparkle like a magical shower of diamonds.

Les Invalides

The best approach to this imposing complex is from the Pont Alexandre III, where spectacular gilded Pegasus statues echo the golden magnificence of the Eglise du Dôme. You'll walk up a grassy esplanade with its grand fountains, chosen by Napoleon to outdo those in Rome. For people with an interest in French military history, a visit to the Army Museum — one of the largest in the world — is a must. Built by Louis XVI as a convalescent hospital for wounded soldiers, the three wings of the building now contain extensive collections of weaponry, uniforms, and war-related paintings. Highlights include the Napoleon rooms and the World War II exhibition in the south wing, but these were closed for refurbishment at the time of writing. There's no scheduled reopening date, so check before you go. You can see Napoleon's mausoleum in the crypt of the beautiful Eglise du Dôme; his remains are encased in six coffins inside a red porphyry sarcophagus set on a massive granite base. Lesser soldiers are remembered in the Soldiers' Church adjoining the Dôme.

Rodin Museum

It's a delight to wander among the massive sculptures in the beautiful gardens of the Musée Rodin, an open-air museum devoted to France's most famous sculptor. You can contemplate his *Penseur (Thinker)*, admire the doughty *Bourgeois du Calais (Burghers of Calais)*, make the acquaintance of the writer Balzac glowering in his dressing gown — survey the scene over a snack in the outdoor café. The elegant Hôtel Biron, where Rodin lived and worked in the final decade of his life, now houses his less weather-resistant works. It traces his artistic evolution through sketches, paintings, and watercolors to his finest sculptures in bronze and marble, including the passionate *Baiser (Kiss)*. There are also works by some of his most notable contemporaries: Renoir, Van Gogh, Monet, and the sculptor's mistress Camille Claudel.

Tarte aux Fruits

When you see the fabulous array of fruit tarts in the windows of pâtisseries like Lenôtre, you might wonder whether it is even worth attempting to make your own, but you won't regret it, especially if you use home-made *pâte sucrée* (sweet pastry) — although of course you can use bought pastry: you'll need 450g/1lb. Use any berries, or a mixture, you like — be creative.

SERVES 8
PREPARATION TIME: 10 MINUTES, PLUS 30 MINUTES CHILLING
COOKING TIME: 30 MINUTES

650g/1lb 7oz mixed summer
   fruits (raspberries,
   blueberries, blackberries,
   or strawberries)
2tbsp sieved raspberry or
   blackberry (bramble) jelly,
   to glaze (optional)

PATE SUCREE:
250g/9oz/2¼ cups all-purpose
   (plain) flour
110g/4oz/½ cup butter, diced
   and slightly softened
110g/4oz/packed 1 cup
   confectioners' (icing) sugar,
   sifted
pinch of salt
2 large eggs

CREME PATISSIERE:
4 large egg yolks
110g/4oz/packed ½ cup
   superfine (caster) sugar
40g/1½oz/⅓ cup all-purpose
   (plain) flour, sifted
510ml/18fl oz/2¼ cups milk
1 vanilla bean (pod), split
   lengthwise

To make the pâte sucrée, mound up the flour on a work surface and make a well in the center. Put in the butter, sugar, and salt and toss lightly to mix. Make another well and add the eggs. Mix with the fingertips of one hand, gradually drawing in the flour with your other hand until the dough is smooth. Knead it a couple of times and roll it into a ball. On a lightly floured surface, roll out the dough to fit a 23-cm/9-inch loose-bottomed fluted tart pan (tin). Line the pan with the dough and trim any excess. Prick the base with a fork and chill for 30 minutes.

Preheat the oven to 200°C/400°F/gas mark 6. Line the pastry case with baking parchment and fill with pie weights (baking beans). Bake blind for 20 minutes, then lower the oven temperature to 180°C/350°F/gas mark 4, remove the parchment and weights (beans), and bake the pastry case for another 5–10 minutes, until crisp and golden. Remove from the oven and allow to cool.

Meanwhile, make the crème pâtissière. Put the egg yolks in a bowl with 50g/2oz/¼ cup of the sugar and whisk to a ribbon consistency. Sift in the flour and mix thoroughly. Heat the milk with the rest of the sugar and the vanilla bean in a saucepan. Just before it boils, pour one-third into the egg mixture, whisking as you go. Pour the mixture back into the pan and bubble gently until thick, stirring continuously. Remove the vanilla bean and pour the crème pâtissière into a bowl. Cover with plastic wrap and leave to cool.

To assemble the tart, stand the base of the pan on a can (of tomatoes, for example) and push off the rim. Leave the pastry case on the base. Give the cold crème pâtissière a stir, then spread it over the pastry case. Top the tart with the fruits, piling them up in the middle. If you want to glaze it, melt the jelly with an equal quantity of water and brush it over the fruit.

Michel Chaudun's Chocolat Chaud à l'Ancienne

Michel Chaudun's real hot chocolate

The ultimate indulgence, steaming hot chocolate made with the very finest real chocolate. Purist chocolatiers like Michel Chaudun think that good chocolate needs no enhancement, but for a different flavor, you could add a little ground cinnamon, grated fresh ginger, or grated orange zest.

SERVES 2
PREPARATION TIME: 5 MINUTES
COOKING TIME: ABOUT 3 MINUTES

400ml/14fl oz/1¾ cups whole milk (or half milk, half heavy whipping cream if you are feeling particularly self-indulgent)

110g/4oz/4 squares best bitter chocolate (70 percent cocoa solids), roughly chopped

60g/2¼oz/⅓ cup superfine (caster) sugar

Gently heat the milk or milk/cream mixture in a small, heavy-bottomed saucepan. When the milk is simmering, drop in the chopped chocolate and stir with a wooden spoon until it has melted. Do not let the milk boil. Stir in the sugar and use a whisk to froth up the hot chocolate. Pour the frothy hot chocolate into two warm mugs and serve immediately.

Pages 158–9: a view of the iconic Eiffel Tower glittering in the night, seen from over the Palais de Chaillot fountains.

Latin Quarter, St-Germain & the Islands

(4th, 5th & 6th arrondissements)

For sheer character and Parisian atmosphere, you can't beat the *Rive Gauche* (Left Bank) of the Seine. The whole area buzzes with life and is full of charm, interest, and history. Moored to the Left Bank "mainland" by a quintet of bridges are two islands, Ile de la Cité and Ile St-Louis. The Ile de la Cité is where Paris began in about 250 BC with the arrival of the Parisii, a colony of Celtic Gauls who settled on the island. By the Middle Ages it had become the center of temporal and spiritual power, with a royal palace at one end (of which only the forbidding Conciergerie and the jewel-like Sainte-Chapelle still survive) and the glorious Gothic cathedral of Notre-Dame at the other.

Latin Quarter, St-Germain & the Islands

(4th, 5th & 6th arrondissements)

Somehow, twelve parishes, together with numerous monasteries and chapels and a network of narrow, bustling streets crammed with houses and businesses, were squeezed into the very small Ile de la Cité. Almost nothing now remains of the medieval city; it was virtually obliterated in the nineteenth century by Georges Eugène Haussmann, who displaced 25,000 people and demolished houses, churches, and ninety streets in pursuit of his grand design for Paris. The only traces left are the secluded square du Vert-Galant and place Dauphine, havens of tranquility and calm in contrast to the frenetic tourist activity of the area around Notre-Dame.

A footbridge links the Ile de la Cité with the tiny Ile St-Louis, a charming if somewhat touristy island which was uninhabited until the seventeenth century, when the architect Louis le Vau built a collection of fabulously elegant town houses there. It's delightful to wander along the tree-lined quays and round the narrow streets, browsing the quirky gift shops and food stores and enjoying a decadently rich ice cream from Berthillon. The myriad bars, tea rooms, cafés, and restaurants offer endless possibilities for rest and refreshment, but choose carefully, as inevitably some are overpriced tourist traps. Be sure to walk to the western tip of the island for a wonderful view of the flying buttresses of Notre-Dame (below).

Paris's intellectual heart beats in the Latin Quarter which has been the city's center of learning since the thirteenth century when the Sorbonne, one of the world's great universities, was founded. The lingua franca of medieval scholars and students was Latin, hence the name, but nowadays in this multi-cultural neighborhood, you are likely to hear just about every language under the sun except Latin. The labyrinth of picturesque cobbled streets and alleyways thrum with student life. Bookshops, jazz clubs, arthouse cinemas, bars, and *boîtes* (nightclubs) jostle for space alongside the historic churches and colleges. There's a genuine bohemian atmosphere, with cafés packed with students engaged in vociferous political and intellectual debate. Cheap eateries are synonymous with student life, and there is no shortage here: Greek tavernas, ethnic restaurants of every kind, fast-food outlets, and bars are all squeezed into the narrow streets. Some are terrific, others less salubrious. The infamous streets just off the place St-Michel are popularly known as *les ruelles de la bactérie* (bacteria alleys), thanks

to their unrefrigerated window displays of doner kebabs and seafood, which attract hungry tourists coming from Notre-Dame in search of sustenance. Far better to bypass the boulevard St-Michel (known to students as the Boul' Mich') and head for the Sorbonne, then venture into the side streets to find more wholesome fare.

The beautiful flower-filled Jardin de Luxembourg forms a tranquil boundary between the Latin Quarter and St-Germain-des-Prés, traditionally the intellectual and literary heart of Paris, where between the wars artists, writers, politicians, and philosophers frequented the famous Café de Flore, Les Deux Magots, and Brasserie Lipp. Today, it's the tourists who gather at these cafés and others like them. The St-Germain area is now more glamorous than intellectual; high-fashion boutiques and luxury food shops have replaced the bookshops and music stores, but it's a paradise for gourmets, fashionistas, and culture vultures alike. For gourmets, the city's most exciting markets and food streets are here; the rue de Buci is a riot of colors and aromas of irresistible produce, seafood, cheeses, and breads — perfect for a picnic to eat in the elegant setting of the Jardin de Luxembourg. If you prefer to feed the mind, where better than Paris's best-loved museum, the wonderful Musée d'Orsay, or the Musée National Eugène Delacroix, home of the Romantic Parisian painter in the tiny, enchanting place Furstenburg? If you just want to soak up the atmosphere, sit at a café opposite Paris's oldest church, St-Germain-des-Prés, and watch Parisian life go by.

Pages 160–1: the ornate marble corridors inside Le Panthéon, the national mausoleum.

163

Debauve et Gallais

This charming old-world shop started as a pharmacy in 1800 and remains almost unchanged, but now it dispenses chocolates instead of drugs. Old-fashioned heavy glass jars on the druggist's counter are filled with chocolate truffles, nutty pralines, and intensely dark chocolate pistoles; even if you buy just two or three, they'll be beautifully wrapped in gold-sealed bags by the sadly surly assistants. Historic chocolates include the original "health" chocolates made with almond milk, and Napoleon's own favorite mixture, an earthy blend with undertones of tobacco.

30 RUE DES STS-PÈRES, 01 45 48 54 67

Berthillon

Whatever the weather, people form queues round the block chez Berthillon for Paris's best ice cream and sorbets. Made with only the purest ingredients, the ice creams are lusciously tasty and decadent with rich colors and equally intense flavors. It's almost impossible to choose between the thirty varieties on offer. Should it be dense, dark bitter chocolate, fragrant *fraises des bois* (wild strawberries), or a seasonal special like melon or lichee? Refreshing sorbets are equally stunning, with a fresh fruitiness that's hard to match, although the poire William granita is a close contender. If you can't face the queues of customers at the main shop, don't despair — plenty of other cafés on the island also sell Berthillon products.

31 RUE ST-LOUIS EN L'ILE,

01 43 54 31 61

Christian Constant

The delightful chocolatier Christian Constant (no relation to the chef of the same name) has a passion for chocolate. He travels the world to source the finest ingredients for his creations and uses a high percentage of cocoa butter for a dense, intense taste. Flavors vary with the seasons; all are delectably aromatic yet subtle. Taster boxes include the most popular choices — pistachio, coffee, ginger, orange blossom, and saffron.

37 RUE D'ASSAS, 01 53 63 15 15

La Ferme des Arènes

Christian Le Lann lovingly matures his cheeses in seventeenth-century cellars on the Ile St-Louis. There's a fabulous selection from all over France, with unusual goat varieties from different regions. Seasonal Tommes de Savoie and Corsican specialties are a treat, and queues form when the rare and delicious new season's Etivaz Gruyère arrives from the Swiss Alps.

60 RUE MONGE, 01 43 36 07 08

Huilerie Artisanale

For four generations, the Leblanc family has produced stone-pressed oils at their traditional mill in Burgundy. They started by making walnut oil from the nuts on a tree in their garden; now they press more than fifteen varieties of fragrant savory oils — olive, pistachio, walnut, pine nut, hazelnut, and many more. Along with oils in distinctive stoneware bottles (some come in travel sizes), you'll find aged vinegars, mustards, and tapenades. It's all very tempting, but be sure to take cash, as credit cards are not accepted.

6 RUE JACOB, 01 46 34 61 55

Librairie Gourmande

If the food in Paris inspires you to rush home and cook, you'll find all the new and second-hand books you need here, from up-to-date cookbooks to rare titles on regional food, wine and spirits, gastronomic studies, and anything else to do with the pleasures of the table. Browse at your leisure (you may find yourself rubbing shoulders with a celebrity chef) or ask the American owner for advice.

4 RUE DANTE, 01 43 54 37 27

Marché Monge

The market stalls at this thrice-weekly (Wednesday, Friday, and Sunday) market are arranged around a lovely fountain. The usual range of seasonal produce is on offer; in the fall, La Pomme Picarde sells farmhouse apple cider as well as a huge variety of apples. The superb selection of hand-made cheeses, yoghurts, and crème fraîche at La Petite Fermière comes direct from the farm, and for something more exotic, the Lebanese traiteur offers subtly spiced goodies.

PLACE MONGE

Pages: 166–7: the Musée d'Orsay, which was once a railway station, contains many priceless exhibits.

Marché Raspail

There's a market every Tuesday and Friday between rue du Cherche-Midi and rue de Rennes, but on Sundays it becomes Paris's biggest and best *marché biologique* (organic market). Whatever you need for a feast, you'll find it here, from poultry and the freshest eggs to artisan cheeses, breads, vegetable tarts, and every kind of root, shoot, and fruit. It's more expensive than the regular market, but the quality is top-notch.

BOULEVARD RASPAIL

Pierre Hermé

The window display of Pierre Hermé's boutique looks more like a jeweler's shop and the master pâtissier's creations certainly sparkle like jewels. Dubbed "the Picasso of pâtisserie" by *Vogue*, portly Pierre Hermé dreams up pastries that he loves to eat himself. They are little works of art with unexpected flavor combinations like hazelnut macaroons with white truffle cream, or Tango, a fusion of sesame seed with parmesan cream, and red bell pepper with raspberry coulis. Like haute couture, the "collection" constantly evolves and prices are shockingly high, but it's hard to resist cakes and pastries that look and taste so exquisite.

72 RUE BONAPARTE, 01 43 54 47 77

Gerard Mulot

Part pâtissier, part traiteur, Gérard Mulot has a loyal following among the residents of St-Germain. Old favorites like delicious coffee-chocolate and fresh fruit tarts or dreamily creamy Paris-Brest are joined by Mulot's signature *mabillon* — crunchy caramel with apricots. Ever-popular clafoutis are made with traditional cherries, or seasonal rhubarb, apples, or summer berries. There's a range of gorgeous chocolates, delicious fruit jellies, and mouthwatering macaroons, with an orange-cinnamon version that many people would kill for. If all this delectable sweetness is too much for you, there is also an appetizing selection of pâtés, hams, and prepared salads to eat with the justly famous sourdough baguettes.

76 RUE DE SEINE, 01 43 26 85 77

Shops in Latin Quarter, St-Germain & the Islands

Poilâne

Lionel Poilâne's daughter continues to oversee the baking of her late lamented father's famous sourdough bread in a traditional wood-fired oven in the boulangerie cellar. Each giant loaf is lovingly formed by hand, left to rise in linen-lined wicker baskets, then baked in the oven to give a chewy center with a crunchy, floury crust. Try to arrive when a fresh batch emerges from the oven — you'll be overwhelmed by the fragrance and, if you are lucky, there'll also be freshly baked croissants, *chaussons de pommes* (apple turnovers), and buttery *punitions* (cookies).
8 RUE DU CHERCHE-MIDI,
01 45 48 42 59

Les Ruchers du Roi

The very best honeys from hives all over France are gathered together in this little shop, an offshoot of its larger sibling in the rue Roi de Sicile. There's an astonishing range, with mandarin blossom and ivy joining the ranks of more familiar lavender and heather, each with its distinctive flavor and subtle aroma. If honey plays a part in a product, you'll find it here, with honey mustard, sticky pain d'épices, beeswax candles, honey-scented soaps, and painted china honey pots.
47 RUE DU CHERCHE-MIDI,
01 42 72 02 96

Sadaharu Aoki

If you're sated with the creamy confections of Parisian pâtisseries and long for something different, you'll find it at this extraordinary Japanese pâtisserie. Familiar creations come with an Asian twist — tea-flavored éclairs with startling green icing; puff pastry napoléons filled with pink cassis and shaped like cherry blossoms with a snowy sprinkling of fleur de sel. Salt and sugar share star billing in black sesame millefeuilles and sushi- and wasabi-flavored macaroons. As you'd expect, everything is exquisitely presented.
35 RUE DE VAUGIRARD, 01 45 44 48 90

La Grande Epicerie

An epicurean tourist attraction in itself, the gargantuan food department of Le Bon Marché department store (in a separate building) is a supermarket par excellence. There's almost nothing a gourmet cannot find here amid the 5,000 different foods from around the world: beautifully displayed mountains of fresh fruit and vegetables, eighty varieties of olive oil, 200 cheeses, fabulously fresh fish, beautiful breads, and a mouth-watering array of cakes and pastries. You'll discover some surprises among the jars of jams and pickles — tangerines in vodka, day lily and apple jelly, and who could resist frogs' legs in pastis sauce? If you're after a picnic, traiteur counters offer traditional terrines and charcuterie alongside exotic and Oriental specialties. Pick up a bottle of chilled white wine from the extensive cellars and enjoy an al fresco lunch in the tiny informal square Boucicaut next door to the store.
LE BON MARCHÉ, 68 RUE DE SÈVRES,
01 44 39 81 00

Restaurants in Latin Quarter, St-Germain & the Islands

Le Bilboquet

Put on your glad rags and head for this famous Left Bank club to enjoy an evening of the best jazz in Paris. Dinner is served in the splendid wood-paneled mezzanine restaurant, complete with copper ceiling, candelabra, and sunken bar. Enjoy classic brasserie dishes like steak, grilled lamb, or simply cooked fish as you listen to modern-day jazz stars in the company, perhaps, of David Bowie or Liza Minelli, who sometimes pop in to enjoy the wonderful atmosphere and high-caliber music when they visit Paris.

13 RUE ST-BENOÎT, 01 45 48 81 84

Brasserie Lipp

This Paris institution is a St-Germain monument to the days when politicians and intellectuals frequented the art-nouveau brasserie. Unsuspecting tourists are shown to the upstairs room, known as "Siberia"; stand firm and insist on a table on the ground floor, or sit on the terrace in the morning sun. Dishes include steak tartare, and impeccably cooked beef and pork platters, with superb pastries from Pierre Hermé and Dallayou to finish — but most people come for the ambience and to remember times past.

151 BOULEVARD ST-GERMAIN,
01 45 48 53 91

L'Epi Dupin

You may have to queue at this tiny, immensely popular bistro near the Bon Marché, but you'll be rewarded with innovative food and interesting flavor combinations that have earned chef-patron François Pasteau a sky-high reputation. Service can be overstretched, so be prepared to sit at your cramped table and munch on freshly baked bread in the shape of a *épi de pai* (wheatsheaf) while you wait for a starter of crisp salad fresh from Rungis market or tongue-tingling caramelized Belgian endive and goat's cheese tart Tatin. Follow with sea bream layered with black pudding, or succulent duck breast. Keep your fingers crossed that the daily choice of six desserts includes chocolate and orange cannelloni. A word of warning — avoid the table at the back right by the loos.

11 RUE DUPIN, 01 42 22 64 56

Chez René

You'll find a little corner of Burgundy in Paris in this simple, cheerful, family-run bistro that offers the kind of food you wish your grandmother had made. Intensely garlicky shrimp or frogs' legs with snail butter might be followed by a vast portion of authentic, tasty coq au vin or a rib-sticking *haricot de mouton* (mutton braised with white beans — served in a black iron pot for you to help yourself). Naturally, boeuf bourguignon features on the menu, along with an *assiette de cochonailles* (every part of the pig, from snout to tail). Those with gargantuan appetites might manage to finish with a chocolate marquise or a palate-cleansing sorbet. It goes without saying that all the wines on the list come from Burgundy.

14 BOULEVARD ST-GERMAIN,
01 43 54 30 23

Restaurants in Latin Quarter, St-Germain & the Islands

Le Comptoir, Hôtel Relais St-Germain

Unfortunately, you can't make a reservation for lunch at this little bistro attached to a charming boutique hotel, but it's the perfect place for a late lunch if you're prepared to take your chance after the midday rush. Choose from a great selection of salads and soups (lobster bisque with cheese ravioli is a star) or a good selection of pâtés, terrines and charcuterie. Classic hot dishes might include seared tuna or lamb stew. The bistro smartens up in the evening and offers a nightly-changing five-course dinner with sophisticated and innovative dishes like spider crab en gelée, millefeuille of beef with foie gras and truffles, and Pyrennean lamb with mushroom ravioli joining the accomplished brasserie favorites.

9 CARREFOUR DE L'ODÉON, 01 44 27 07 997

Mon Vieil Ami

Avoid the indifferent tourist traps and head for this hugely popular modern bistro, where you are assured of a friendly welcome from the Anglophone waiters and accomplished, deeply satisfying cooking. The closely packed tables in the simple beamed room make for a convivial atmosphere, and it's good to peruse what your neighbors are eating before choosing from the shortish menu of tempting dishes like meltingly tender shoulder of lamb braised with root vegetables and Moroccan spices, caramelized choucroûte, or free-range chicken with pig's head stuffing and wild mushrooms. Desserts are equally delicious, with a heavenly chocolate tart as a highlight.

69 RUE ST-LOUIS EN L'ILE, 01 40 46 01 35

Les Papilles

Choose your wine from an interesting selection of more than 400 varieties and drink it with your lunch or dinner at this delightful, welcoming bistro-cum-food-and-wine shop. *Les Papilles* means "tastebuds" and yours will be tickled by the quality charcuterie and fresh salads chosen from the traiteur counter at the front of the store, or seasonal plats du jour like cream of artichoke soup, braised shoulder of veal, and rich chocolate ganache or panna cotta with wild strawberries. Wines are available by the glass and the owners will happily open a new bottle for you if there's something special you want to try.

30 RUE GAY LUSSAC, 01 43 25 20 79

Le Petit Pontoise

Unusual ingredients add spice and invention to the menu at this intimate little bistro, whose chef-patron trained at La Tour d'Argent. Elements of haute cuisine creep into the menu, with *parmentier de canard au foie gras* (duck with potatoes and unctuous foie gras), but most of the cooking offers surprise elements like roast kid on pain d'épices, or Thai-style scallops with a lime and cilantro (coriander) kick. Floating islands with pink praliné are a treat, or there's chocolate *Amadeus*, a version of a soft-centered layered chocolate mousse cake for chocoholics. Friendly service adds to the charm.

9 RUE PONTOISE, 01 43 29 25 20

Procope

Dating from 1686, this atmospheric bistro is the oldest in Paris; the original Italian *padrone* (patron) Francesco Procopio, was the first person to introduce a new-fangled brew called coffee to the gastronomes of France. Over the centuries, the world's great politicians, writers, and philosophers have gathered here to put the world to rights; even today, a table is still reserved in case the French president drops by. The menu offers no surprises, with boeuf bourguignon, civet of duckling, and similar hearty bistro fare. The real reason to come here is to eat in the plush red-and-gold downstairs room with its magnificent chandeliers, or climb the creaking wooden stairs to the sumptuous mirrored dining room hung with historic paintings and boasting a regal fleur-de-lys carpet.

13 RUE DE L'ANCIENNE COMÉDIE, 01 40 46 79 00

La Tour d'Argent

It costs a king's ransom to eat here but it's worth it for the magical view of Notre-Dame and the Seine from this grande dame of Paris restaurants. Food from another era includes the signature *canard à la presse* (pressed duck), with its unctuous jus enriched with Cognac, Madeira and foie gras; if you order this or the equally famous duckling à l'orange, you are given a postcard to mark the occasion. And the octogenarian owner ensures that a meal here is an occasion, from the seamless if somewhat stuffy service to the featherlight lobster quenelles, and flambéed peaches in framboise liqueur. A visit to the legendary wine cellar, which has more than half a million bottles, offers a rare treat. For an affordable once-in-a-lifetime treat, go for the prix-fixe lunch.

15–17 QUAI DE TOURNELLE,
01 43 54 23 31

Le Reminet

One of the few Left Bank bistros to open on weekends (it closes on Tuesdays and Wednesdays instead), the tiny, cramped Le Reminet is a favorite place for Sunday lunch. Using the freshest ingredients, Hugues Gournay creates refined dishes with a modern twist. Sea-fresh fish is a delight; skate braised with baby fennel are unusual and delicious. Carnivores can indulge in salt-marsh lamb from Normandy or immaculately cooked beef with shallot purée. Whatever you do, leave room for one of the irresistible desserts like coffee meringue with extra bitter chocolate mousse and espresso jelly. The weekday lunch menu is one of Paris's greatest bargains.

3 RUE DES GRANDS-DEGRÉS,
01 44 07 04 24

Le Timbre

British-born Chris Wright's diminutive bistro is popular among Left Bank gastronomes. It may be small, but the output from his cupboard-sized kitchen is impressive. The weekly changing blackboard menu might offer *croustillant de boudin noir aux oignons confits* (crispy black pudding with confit onions), *palombe rôti aux marrons* (succulent roast wood pigeon with chestnuts), or fresh fish from the nearby Poissonerie du Dôme. British imposters like mushy peas or mint sauce make occasional accompaniments to the resolutely francophile dishes, but there's always "le vrai" fromage anglais to finish your meal if you don't fancy the superlative *millefeuille du Timbre*, assembled before your eyes, with its airy puff pastry top emblazoned with a signature 'T'. Bilingual service is friendly and Le Timbre is a welcoming haven for solo diners.

3 RUE STE BEUVE 6E, 01 45 49 10 40

Pages 172–3: a view of Notre-Dame Cathedral, with the Pont Tournelle spanning the River Seine below.

Palombe aux Céleris et Marrons

Squab with celery and chestnuts

This dish featured on the menu the day that I went for lunch at Le Timbre. I loved the contrast of the sweet creamy sauce with the savory squab and crunch of the bright green celery.

SERVES 4
PREPARATION TIME: 30 MINUTES
COOKING TIME: 20 MINUTES

4 fat squab
1¾ pints/1 liter/4½ cups chicken stock
salt and freshly ground black pepper
2–3tbsp olive oil

350g/12oz green celery, sliced diagonally into 5-mm/¼-inch slices
60g/2½oz vacuum-packed chestnuts
120ml/4fl oz/½ cup heavy (double) cream

Preheat the oven to 200ºC/400ºF/gas mark 6. Put the squab in a wide pan, cover with the chicken stock, and bring to a boil. Lower the heat and poach for about 5 minutes, then lift out the squab and leave until cool enough to handle. Reserve the stock. Cut off the squab breasts and legs and remove their bones. Season the squab pieces, put them in a roasting pan, drizzle with oil, and roast for 10 minutes.

Meanwhile, put the celery in a soufflé dish with the chestnuts. The dish should only be large enough to hold the celery and chestnuts in a snug layer. Pour in just enough of the reserved stock to cover them. This method ensures that you will use just the right amount of stock. Pour everything into a saucepan and reduce over a high heat until almost all the stock has evaporated, then stir in the cream and warm through.

Arrange the squab breasts and legs on warm plates and spoon the celery, chestnuts, and sauce on top.

Potage St-Germain

Pea soup

Traditionally, dried (marrowfat) peas were used to thicken this soup, but it has a much more delicate, sweet flavor if made with fresh peas and potatoes. If you use frozen peas, you can leave out the blanching process.

SERVES 4
PREPARATION TIME: 15 MINUTES
COOKING TIME: 25 MINUTES

600g/1lb 5oz peas in the pod, or 250g/9oz/1¾ cups frozen petits pois
25g/1oz/2tbsp butter
110g/4oz potatoes, peeled and cut into 2.5-cm/1-inch chunks
1¾ pints/1 liter/4½ cups chicken stock or water

salt and freshly ground white pepper
50ml/2fl oz/¼ cup heavy (double) cream, lightly whipped
4 small sprigs of fresh mint

Shell the peas, drop them into a pan of boiling water for 1 minute to blanch them, then drain. Reserving 2 tablespoons of peas for the garnish, put the rest in a saucepan with the butter, and sweat them over a medium heat for 2 minutes. Add the potatoes, stir, pour in the stock or water and bring to a boil. Reduce the heat and simmer for about 20 minutes until the potatoes are soft, then, using a blender or food processor, purée the contents of the pan until they reach a smooth consistency.

Season the soup to taste, stir in the cream and reserved peas, and ladle the soup into warm bowls. Garnish each bowl of soup with a mint sprig.

Landmarks

After you have wandered through the narrow historic streets of the Latin Quarter, mingled with the crowds of students, and devoured its abundance of bistros and cafés, you'll have worked up the stamina to enjoy the cultural delights the area: the striking neo-classical grandeur of the Panthéon, the impressionists and post-impressionists of the Musée d'Orsay, the elegant and superbly landscaped Jardin de Luxembourg, and, of course, the awe-inspiring Notre-Dame. If you time your visit just before sunset, you'll experience the palpable sense of anticipation as the lights are gradually turned on in the cathedral and people gather to worship.

Jardin de Luxembourg

One of the oldest and most elegant parks in Paris, the Jardin de Luxembourg (below left) is a wonderful oasis to restore the soul after the hustle and bustle of the Latin Quarter and St-Germain. You'll rarely find yourself alone here, as it is everyone's favorite meeting place, but there's always a quiet corner somewhere among the mixture of formal and informal gardens with trees, immaculate lawns, colorful flowerbeds, wide gravel paths, fountains, and a puppet theater. Sit by the central octagonal pond and gaze at Marie de' Medici's Italianate Palais de Luxembourg (now the seat of the French Senate), or wander along to the baroque Medici Fountain, with its grotto and statue of the malevolent Polyphemos hurling a rock at the lovers Acis and Galatea.

Musée d'Orsay

If you have time to visit only one museum while you are in Paris, make it this one. Under the monumental iron-and-glass roof of the dramatically renovated Gare d'Orsay railway station, there's a feast of art and design spanning the years from 1848 to 1914, including a stupendous collection of impressionists and post-impressionists. All the exhibits from sculpture and astonishing art nouveau furniture and decorative arts, to paintings, photography and much more, deserve attention, but the building is a major attraction in its own right, with a statue-lined promenade running the full length of the vast main hall and the two massive station clocks. One provides the backdrop for the Café des Hauteurs on the fifth floor. Take a break from the vision of the impressionist painters and gaze through the glass clock face at the view of modern Paris.

Notre-Dame de Paris

The mass of tourists may detract from its splendor and spirituality, but no one could fail to be impressed and inspired by the grandeur of this magnificent Gothic cathedral with its sculpture-encrusted twin-towered facade (there are twenty-eight statues on the west front alone), delicate flying buttresses, and massive rose windows. Commissioned by the Bishop of Paris in 1160 to replace two crumbling churches that stood on the site once occupied by a Gallo-Roman temple to Jupiter, the cathedral was finally completed in 1345 and has dominated the Ile de la Cité and the Seine ever since. During the Revolution, it was plundered by the mob, who tore down and decapitated the statues of the kings of Judaea, wrongly supposing them to be kings of France. By the nineteenth century, the cathedral had become so dilapidated that it was briefly abandoned, but largely thanks to the efforts of Victor Hugo and the success of *The Hunchback of Notre-Dame*, enough money was raised to restore it to its former glory.

The vast interior of Notre-Dame is as impressive as the facade, with graceful columns, a nave that soars up to the heavens, and truly glorious stained-glass windows that shower the nave with shimmering multicolored light when the sunlight filters through them. Great moments in history have taken place here, including the coronation of the English king Henry VI, Napoleon's crowning of himself as Emperor, and the beatification of Jeanne d'Arc. The best way to appreciate the extraordinary masonry is to climb the 387 steps to the top of the towers, where you'll come face to face with the grotesque gargoyles that stand atop the cathedral.

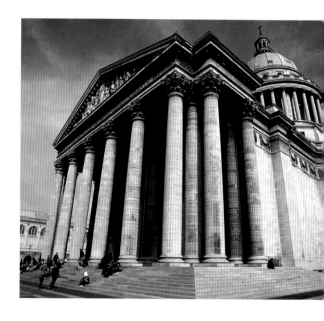

Le Panthéon

This massive neo-classical domed basilica (above), based on the Pantheon in Rome, towers above the narrow alleyways of the Latin Quarter. It was commissioned by Louis XV to thank Saint Geneviève, patron saint of Paris, for his remarkable recovery from a near-fatal illness, but by the time it was finished, in 1789, the king had been dead for fifteen years. Just two years later, in 1791, revolutionaries seized the building, all Christian references were removed, and the church was rededicated as a "temple of reason" to the great Frenchmen of the age of liberty. The austere crypt became a mausoleum for such heroes as Voltaire, Victor Hugo, Emile Zola, and Louis Braille, inventor of the Braille reading system. In 1995, Marie Curie's remains were brought here, the first woman to be buried in the Panthéon for her own achievements. To be "pantheonized" is one of the greatest accolades in France, and the question of who merits reburial here is still cause for much heated debate. Look up into the dome to see where Foucault hung his pendulum to prove that the earth rotates on its axis; a replica hangs here now.

Salade aux Endives, Roquefort et Noix
Belgian endive, Roquefort, and walnut salad

This classic bistro salad is a perfect combination of three ingredients: Belgian endive for crunch, walnuts for bite, and tangy Roquefort cheese. If you prefer, use other bitter leaves like frisée or escarole instead of Belgian endive.

SERVES 4
PREPARATION TIME: 5 MINUTES

2 heads of Belgian endive
(white, red, or a combination
of both)
16 freshly shelled walnuts,
halved, or 32 walnut halves
110g/4oz Roquefort cheese

VINAIGRETTE:
1½tbsp tarragon or white
wine vinegar
1tsp Dijon mustard
salt and freshly ground
black pepper
3tbsp sunflower or olive oil
2tbsp walnut oil

First make the vinaigrette. Put the vinegar, mustard, and a little salt and pepper in a bowl, and whisk until smooth. Add the oils and whisk lightly until blended.

Separate the Belgian endive leaves, then wash and pat them dry. Halve any large leaves lengthwise. Place the leaves in a salad bowl, add the walnuts, and crumble in the Roquefort in fairly large pieces. Pour on the vinaigrette, toss the salad, and serve.

Sablés au Chocolat
Chocolate shortbread (cookies)

Parisian pâtissiers offer such an irresistible choice of shortbread and pastries that you can buy anything you want, but sometimes it's fun to make your own. These crumbly sablés are perfect to nibble with a cup of coffee or hot chocolate, but also make a great dessert half-dipped in bitter (70 percent cocoa solids) chocolate and served with a chocolate sorbet or vanilla ice cream.

MAKES ABOUT 36
PREPARATION TIME: 5 MINUTES PLUS CHILLING
COOKING TIME: 15 MINUTES

250g/9oz/2¼ cups all-purpose
(plain) flour
25g/1oz/⅓ cup cocoa powder
250g/9oz/heaped 1 cup
unsalted butter, at room
temperature, diced

95g/3½oz/¾ cup confectioners'
(icing) sugar
1 large egg white
110g/4oz/4 squares
bittersweet (70 percent
cocoa solids) chocolate,
melted (optional)

Sift the flour and cocoa powder into a bowl. Put the butter in another bowl and, using a hand-held electric mixer, beat until pale and fluffy. Sift the confectioners' sugar over the butter, add the egg white, and beat for 1 minute until well amalgamated. Add the sifted flour and cocoa mixture and mix at low speed until just incorporated. Cover the bowl with plastic wrap and chill until the dough is firm.

Lay the dough on a sheet of plastic wrap or baking parchment and roll it into a cylinder about 4cm/1½ inches in diameter. Wrap it tightly and refrigerate again until firm.

Preheat the oven to 180°C/350°F/gas mark 4. Cut the dough into 1-cm/½-inch slices and place on a baking sheet lined with baking parchment, spacing them well apart. Bake for 12–15 minutes until firm. Cool on a wire rack and serve the sablés either as they are, or dip one half of each in melted chocolate and leave to set on a sheet of baking parchment.

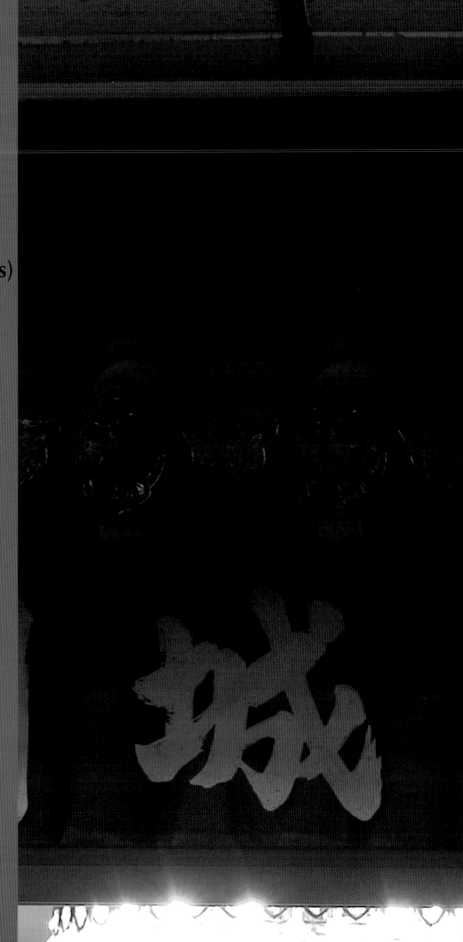

Place d'Italie & Montparnasse

(13th, 14th & 15th arrondissements)

The place d'Italie forms the axis of an area of two contrasting halves. No one could call the triangular neighborhood between place d'Italie and avenue d'Ivry the most beautiful part of Paris, with its rather brutal landscape of 1960s gray concrete high-rise blocks, but it thrums with a vibrant personality unlike anywhere else in Paris. This is Chinatown (the word is the same in French), a sort of Hong Kong-sur-Seine, where everything has an Asian flavor, from the enigmatic Chinese characters on the facades of the fast-food restaurants, to the gourmet riches of the vast Tang Frères grocery empire.

Place d'Italie & Montparnasse
(13th, 14th & 15th arrondissements)

It might, perhaps, be more accurate to call this "Asian" quarter; although the Chinese community makes up eighty percent of the population, the area is also home to a diverse society of Cambodians, Vietnamese, Laotians, and Thais, whose cultures combine to create a Far Eastern world of color and exoticism. For most of the year, the communities lead separate lives, following their own cultures and traditions, but at Chinese New Year they converge in the streets to celebrate with a riot of exploding fireworks, spectacular dancing dragons, and showers of rice rain.

Walk along any road around place d'Italie and you'd think yourself in Asia. Wafts of fragrant rice, pho containing noodles and fresh vegetables, wok-fried vegetables, or toasted sesame oil drift out from the 150 Asian restaurants that are crammed into this single small area. Old women in Mao jackets totter along the street, weighed down with bulging bags of exotic fruit, vegetables, fish, spices, and steamed buns from the Asian pâtisseries, while knots of men study the myriad colorful notices on the wall beside the Tang emporium. Music stores emit tinny Asian music, Chinese barbers and hairdressers wield their scissors, and if you need cash, endless money-changers offer attractive rates.

The grim gray esplanade of the Olympiades tower blocks hides another multitude of Chinese emporia and restaurants. From silk fashions to sewing machines and karaoke machines — if you want it, they've got it. At street level, the ground-floor buildings look like a mass of short pagodas with typical wavy roofs. But it is a happy coincidence, given that the complex was built in 1965, well before the influx of the Asian population, and the rooftops were never intended to mimic Buddhist temples. Inspired by the nearby place de Vénétie, they are, instead, meant to resemble waves on the choppy Grand Canal in Venice, but have been adopted by the Asiatic communities to be a symbol of harmony.

By contrast, the pretty cobbled streets and picturesque old houses of the Butte aux Cailles (Hill of the Quails), north of rue de Tolbiac, retain a refreshing village charm. The Butte has escaped modern development, thanks to the network of ancient quarries under the hill that make it impossible to erect multi-storey buildings. The working watermills that once powered the local tanning industry along the River Bièvre disappeared in the nineteenth century, when the river became so polluted by the cochineal-dye industry that it had to be covered up. With no industry, the area sank into deprivation and such poverty that the residents had to resort to eating horsemeat. France's first *boucherie chevaline* (horsemeat butcher's shop) opened in the place d'Italie in 1866. In recent years the Butte has been rejuvenated and enlivened by a new, young population, but the bucolic atmosphere of the steep, winding streets still remains, at least by day. At night, the area suddenly wakes up, with numerous bars and inexpensive bistros

throbbing with music, and youthful customers spilling out into the narrow alleyways.

Just west of the Butte aux Cailles is Montparnasse, which once boasted a butte of its own, on whose peak students aped the ancient Greek poets by declaiming poetic works, hence the name Mont Parnasse (Mount Parnassus). The hill had crumbled away by the eighteenth century, but this didn't bother artists and bohemians like Modigliani, Utrillo, Picasso, and a host of others, who decamped to Montparnasse as rents rose sky high in Montmartre. Chagall and other refugees fleeing the Russian Revolution, followed, then came a wave of American writers, artists, and free-thinkers. The area proliferated with artists' studios, cafés, and bohemian bars with rather dubious reputations.

Sadly, bohemian Montparnasse has long gone. With the dramatic destruction of the old railway station by a runaway train bursting through the first floor of the elegant facade, and the uninspired rebuilding that followed, the atmosphere of the old artistic neighborhood gave way to a largely concrete commercial center, dominated by Paris's first skyscraper, the unlovely Tour Montparnasse. And yet, amid all the concrete and the sordid sex shops, the area still has an animated feel with its lively fringe theaters and global restaurants and bars.

Pages 180–1: if you're feeling in the mood to cook or eat Asian food, the area around place d'Italie offers restaurants and Chinese grocery stores galore.

Shops in Place d'Italie & Montparnasse

Les Abeilles

Apiarists swarm to Jean-Jacques Schakmundès's tiny shop devoted to honey and the art of bee-keeping. There are jars of honey from his hives at the foot of the Butte aux Cailles, and forty-five other varieties from all over France and far-flung countries. Flavors depend on the season; rarities include crystaline bell heather honey and bourdaine, made from a herb that cures stomach complaints. If the range of honeys is not enough, there are honey sweets, mustards, oils, soaps, and home-made pain d'épices, plus medicaments and royal jelly.

21 BUTTE AUX CAILLES,
01 45 81 43 48

Baillardrun

If you yearn for authentic *cannelés* (little fluted cakes) from Bordeaux but can't make the journey there, go no further than the Gare Montparnasse. Twice daily, consignments of these sticky specialties arrive on the train from Bordeaux and are rushed to the pâtisserie, still warm from the oven, crusty on the outside and soft in the middle. As each batch arrives, there's a stampede to Baillardrun to purchase them at the peak of perfection.

GARE PARIS MONTPARNASSE, DEPARTURE LEVEL C (OPPOSITE PLATFORM 13),
01 40 47 99 24

Boucherie Desnoyer – Régalez Vous

Who would believe that a butcher's window display could be a work of art? To Hugo Desnoyer, all his meat is a thing of beauty, from the succulent Lozère lamb, grazed on pastures of clover and pimpernel, to robust, long-matured Salers beef. Everything is immaculately sourced and star chefs from haute cuisine kitchens such as l'Ambroisie and Pierre Gagnaire, and the president himself, flock to buy their meat at this little shop. Alongside haunches of beef and fillets of milk-fed veal, you'll find ready-stuffed roasts, like rosettes of veal with ham and cheese, pork with dried fruits, or chickens with truffles or earthy ceps and chestnuts in the fall, and Desnoyer's award-winning boudin noir.

25 RUE MOUTON DUVERNET,
01 45 40 76 67

Daguerre Marée

Eighty different kinds of freshwater and sea fish and weird and wonderful shellfish arrive fresh every day at this poissonnerie, which is more like an aquarium than a fish shop. Choose from half a dozen varieties of fresh oysters, or razor clams, mussels, and live crustaceans; they're all cleaned and ready for you to take home and cook.

9 RUE DAGUERRE, 01 43 22 13 52

Fromagerie Lasnier

The Lasnier family has been running their traditional neighborhood fromagerie for three generations and the pride they take in their products is obvious. Cheeses are at the peak of perfection, and for those with a sweet tooth, there are home-made pastries and cakes.

51 RUE DE TOLBIAC, 01 45 83 03 30

Fromage Rouge

If you love goats' cheese, you'll adore this little fromagerie for its huge array of chèvre specimens. There's a bar at the back of the shop for tastings, or sit and enjoy a plate of cheeses or a convivial fondue washed down with one of the carefully chosen wines.

8 RUE DELAMBRE, 01 42 79 00 40

Inno

For one-stop food shopping you can't do better than a visit to the cavernous Inno, an upmarket Monoprix superstore, where you'll find an eye-popping range of fresh and prepared foods. Alongside standard supermarket staples are charcuterie and cheese counters, pâtisseries and appetizing traiteur dishes to reheat at home. The wines section is impressive and the store open until late.

31–35 RUE DU DÉPART, 01 42 79 80 42

L'Empire des Thés

Decorated like a sumptuous Chinese lacquered cabinet, this elegant emporium is a restful haven from the frenetic street life outside. The 200 delicate teas with evocative names span the world, from Asia to South America. The bewildering choice is catalogued by color and region like a wine list, and includes rare white *aiguilles d'argent* (silver needles) and plum flower, green, blue-green, red, and black, and flowery, flavored, and sleep-inducing leaves. Knowledgeable staff will guide you through the maze of choice, or you can sit and enjoy a tea-tasting with a selection of fragrant teas and, of course, delicate tea-flavored cake. You'll be tempted to buy the range of unusual and beautiful teapots and bowls for serving and drinking your tea.

101 AVENUE D'IVRY, 01 45 85 66 33

Au Jardin des Plantes

You won't find better quality, fresher organic fruit and vegetables anywhere than in this vegetarian's paradise. All the produce sold in this huge mini-market is locally grown, and the riot of colorful salads and aromatic herbs is a joy for the eyes and the nose.

50 RUE DES PLANTES,
01 45 77 70 14

Maison des Bonbons

Step back into your childhood at this old-fashioned candy shop with its confections that grandmère would have adored. Crystalized rose petals and verbena, candied violets, licorice and marshmallows...If you're a child at heart, you'll find it hard to resist all the wonderful candies sold in this shop.

14 RUE MOUTON DUVERNET,
01 45 41 25 55

Marché Edgar-Quinet

On Wednesday and Saturday mornings, this large market stretches along the boulevard next to the Montparnasse cemetery. There's the usual splendid array of seasonal produce, with traiteurs, fish stalls, fresh farm cheeses, and delicious artisan breads.

TERRE-PLAINS DU BOULEVARD EDGAR-QUINET

Moulin de la Vierge

The original and most delightful of Basile Kamir's small chain of bakeries, this once-abandoned 1900s boulangerie was threatened with demolition if no one continued the bread-making business. Music promoter Kamir rose to the challenge and learnt the art of baking the heavenly sourdough breads for which he's now famous. The aroma of naturally leavened baguettes and boules, olive and anchovy fougasses, and sweet puff-pastry palmiers and tartes Tatin baking in the old wood-fired oven is truly divine.

105 RUE VERCINGÉTORIX,
01 45 43 09 84

Shops in Place d'Italie & Montparnasse

Nouveau Yv Nghy

The range of Chinese and Vietnamese pastries is astonishing at what may well be the best Asian pâtisserie in Paris. Freshly baked treats at very low prices include *boules de neige* (featherlight steamed "snowballs") filled with soy bean, coconut, or peanut paste, and Vietnamese cakes squishy with lotus or durian cream. Try the coconut croissants, or sink your teeth into the sesame-coated nougat.

67 AVENUE D'IVRY, 01 45 86 93 36

Pâtisserie de Saison

Everything looks so tempting at this little Asian pastry shop, from the vibrant-green, moist-steamed pistachio cake to the tangy, light-as-air lemon and almond sponges, and the crisp-flaky croissants with a filling of lotus or soy bean paste. Other delights include sweet steamed cakes, like steamed coconut buns with peanut or sesame paste, and pistachio cake — different and delicious.

2 RUE SIMONE WEIL, 01 45 84 37 70

Poissonnerie du Dôme

A favorite of chefs and restaurateurs, this wonderful blue-and-white-tiled fish shop sells stupendously fresh fish, some straight from the Breton boats. Giant crabs, succulent scallops, wild salmon from the Loire, turbot and sole so fresh that they're almost still flapping; none of these comes cheap, but the quality justifies the high prices.

4 RUE DELAMBRE, 01 43 35 23 95

Tang Frères

For a colorful, authentic Asian experience, a visit to the gigantic Tang Frères grocery store — really more like a village — is a must. Ten thousand people shop here every day for produce from the entire Asian continent. Counters spill over with exotic fruit and vegetables: hairy rambutans, jewel-like kumquats, and bulbs of bok choy. There's a bewildering range of spiced oils and sauces — soy bean paste, black bean, chilli, plus shrimp crackers, noodles, and wonton wrappers. If it's Asian and edible, you'll find it here. Live carp are on offer, plus seaweed, huge bags of rice, frozen wontons, and dried mushrooms, alongside conventional grocery store fare. No need to worry about the wherewithal to cook and eat your purchases. Just browse the aisles of chopsticks, woks, steamers, and decorative bowls.

If you're hungry for some Asian takeout food, visit the separate, neighboring Tang Gourmet, where you will find lacquered Chinese ducks and spit-roasted spare ribs hung in their burnished glory above Asian traiteur counters for fast food with a difference.

48 AVENUE D'IVRY, 01 45 70 80 00

Pages 186–7: the markets trumpet their competive prices for fresh exotic produce.

Restaurants in Place d'Italie & Montparnasse

Le Bambou

The surroundings are sober, but Parisians flock to this popular restaurant for some of the best authentic Vietnamese cuisine in the city. Choose from a dozen different soups, noodles with grilled beef or pork, and exceptionally fresh spring rolls and steamed ravioli. Service is efficient and prices low. Vietnamese families love to come here for a convivial weekend lunch, so be prepared to queue for a table.

70 RUE BAUDRICOURT, 01 45 70 91 75

La Cerisaie

Eating at this tiny bistro is like being en famille in someone's home. Top-class offerings include silky wild-boar rillettes, and shoulder of lamb cooked with root vegetables for seven hours until tender enough to eat with a spoon. Goose breast comes with roasted figs, which also make an appearance in a crumble. Chocolate fondant with coffee ice cream is sheer delight.

70 BOULEVARD EDGAR-QUINET, 01 43 20 98 98

Chez Paul

The modern exterior belies the traditional décor and cooking of this popular neighborhood restaurant. More serious and sober than its funky neighbors, it offers robust bistro fare, with lyonnais specialties like ham slow-braised to succulent perfection in hay, or *tablier de sapeur* (surprisingly delicious slabs of breaded tripe). Other main dishes include rack of lamb and veal kidneys, which are served with potato purée. Gorgeous desserts follow the hefty trend.

22 RUE DE LA BUTTE AUX CAILLES, 01 45 89 22 11

Restaurants in Place d'Italie & Montparnasse

La Coupole

Now part of the impressive Flo chain of brasseries, cavernous La Coupole has retained all its 1920s glamour, with its art-deco pillars, cubist floor tiles, and paintings by different artists from the early twentieth century to the present day. Oysters and other superbly fresh shellfish and crustaceans are piled on the long counter; make your own selection of briny oysters, spider crabs, or langoustines, or feast on a plâteau de fruits de mer. The menu features brasserie classics like steak tartare and choucroûte, along with steak and unexpected curries. Hot-fudge sundaes are a special treat.

102 BOULEVARD DU MONTPARNASSE, 01 43 20 14 20

Le Dôme

Another iconic 1900s Parisian brasserie complete with colorful Tiffany lamps and a mass of potted plants, whose celebrity clientèle is outshone by the spectacularly good fish and shellfish. Oysters are ultra-fresh, sole is immaculate, and the home-salted cod with a garlic aïoli is superb. Finish with some fine cheese from the Auvergne.

108 BOULEVARD DU MONTPARNASSE, 01 43 35 25 81

Au Petit Cahoua

Couscous is the star at this little North African oasis, whose tented interior and painted pottery tagines instantly put you in the mood for some of its delicately spiced specialties, like the ratatouille that accompanies meltingly tender *méchoui* (lamb). Generous portions of garnished couscous are preceded by crisp briks and vegetable fritters, and pigeon *b'stilla* is a savory marriage of meat and crisp, sugary pastry. If you've room, Moroccan pastries are sweet and sticky. Finish with fresh mint tea.

39 BOULEVARD ST-MARCEL, 01 47 07 24 42

Au Petit Marguéry

The food is traditional as the décor in this attractive turn-of-the-twentieth-century brasserie with its deep pink walls, antique tiles, and etched glass. Game is a specialty; in season you'll find grouse, partridge, wild boar, and a classic *lièvre à la royale* (hare stewed in its own blood). If all this sounds too hefty, try the ravioli with sea scallops, or rascasse with tapenade. To finish, airy Grand Marnier soufflé is the house specialty.

9 BOULEVARD DE PORT-ROYAL, 01 43 31 58 59

Pho Banh Cuon

The *pho* (soup with rice noodles and fresh vegetables) is the main attraction at this unprepossessing-looking Vietnamese restaurant. Considered the best in Paris, a copious and flavorful bowl of special Tonkinoise pho with dumplings or chicken and a mountain of crisp beansprouts and colorful crudités will fill you up and leave you happy for very little outlay.

129 AVENUE DE CHOISY, 01 45 83 61 15

La Régalade

Régaler means "treat" and you'll certainly have that at Bruno Doucet's La Régalade. The décor is comfortable and cozy, and set menus (the only option, along with blackboard specials, which change with the seasons) are reasonable. A whole country terrine is brought to the table before you order a seasonal special — asparagus, wild mushrooms, or game — and you can choose from turbot with fresh petits pois, or gargantuan duckling with a generous portion of foie gras (for two). The Provençal apricot tart and wild strawberry sablé are superb. Be sure to reserve.

49 AVENUE JEAN MOULIN,
01 45 45 68 58

Le Temps des Cerises

Cell phones aren't allowed at this co-operative restaurant, where shared tables add to the comradely atmosphere in the old fashioned dining room. There's nothing chic about the food — just flavorful, good honest fare at low prices. Set menus might include andouillette, skirt of beef with roquefort, or blood sausage with apples.

18 RUE DE LA BUTTE AUX CAILLES,
01 45 89 69 48

Le Tonkinoise

Ignore the stark interior and tuck into the refined food at one of Paris's finest Vietnamese restaurants. Stuffed whelks are an unexpected treat, or try the monkfish or catfish with caramelized palm sugar. Spring rolls are crisp and delicious, the ravioli succulent, and salads include crunchy and unusual ingredients like lotus root. Flavors are pungent and aromatic, and dishes include noodles or rice, making a meal here an inexpensive pleasure.

20 RUE PHILIBERT LOCUT,
01 45 85 98 98

Vin et Marée

The gorgeous red-plush banquettes and exuberant mural are reminiscent of an Indian restaurant, but what you'll get here is outstanding fresh seafood brought every night from Rungis market and cooked with a light touch to preserve its flavor. Creative dishes include lobster with bacon, or try the supremely tender tuna steak, or tiny slips (baby sole). The rum baba is large enough to share with friends, but it's so delicious that you may not want to.

108 AVENUE DU MAINE, 01 43 20 29 50

Pho Tai

Rare beef pho

It may seem odd to include a Vietnamese recipe in a book about Parisian food, but the French will happily cross the city to eat a good pho (pronouced "fer"), Vietnamese noodle soup, in Chinatown. A special beef pho contains rare steak, well-done flank, beef tendon, tripe, and meatballs; this is a simpler version to make at home.

SERVES 6
PREPARATION TIME: 30 MINUTES
COOKING TIME: 1¼ HOURS

380g/13½oz thin *ban pho* (rice stick) noodles, or Chinese rice noodles

175g/6oz beef fillet or sirloin, frozen for about 20 minutes (this makes it easier to slice thinly)

handful of cilantro (coriander leaves)

4 scallions (spring onions), thinly sliced

SPICED BEEF BROTH:
1 large onion, peeled and very thickly sliced

1 carrot, thickly sliced

1 rutabaga (turnip), thickly sliced

5cm/2-inch piece of ginger root, unpeeled and halved lengthwise

2–3 bird's eye or other chilies, deseeded and thinly sliced

1.75 liters/3 pints/7½ cups good beef stock (don't use a bouillon cube)

1 beef bone or 250g/9oz beef flank or cheap stewing cut

3–4 star anise

3 cloves

8cm/3 inch cinnamon stick

1–2 tbsp *nuoc mam* (fish sauce)

2cm/¾-inch piece of jaggery (palm sugar) or 1tsp soft brown sugar

GARNISHES:
175g/6oz beansprouts

12 sprigs of fresh mint

3 limes, cut into wedges

To make the broth, heat a skillet (frying) or griddle pan until very hot, put in the onion, carrot, rutabaga, and ginger, and lightly char them all over. Transfer them to a large saucepan with the chilies, pour in the beef stock, and add the bone or beef flank. Set over a medium heat.

Return the skillet to the heat, add the star anise, cloves, and cinnamon, toast briefly until they smell very aromatic, then add them to the broth. Bring to a boil, lower the heat, and simmer for about 1 hour. Remove the vegetables, aromatics, and bone or flank, and add the fish sauce to the broth. The fish sauce is very salty, so taste the broth to judge whether you need 1 or 2 tablespoons of the jaggery and keep the broth at just below simmering point.

Cook the ban pho according to the directions on the packet, then drain and put them in a bowl.

Slice the semi-frozen beef across the grain as thinly as possible. If you want a mixture of textures, thinly slice the flank, if used, as well.

To serve the pho, divide the noodles among six warmed large soup bowls, lay the slices of beef on top and scatter with the cilantro and scallions. Ladle in the hot broth (the raw beef will cook to rare in the heat) and let everyone help themselves to the garnishes.

Raie au Beurre Noir et aux Câpres

Skate with black butter and capers

The secret of this classic dish is to ensure that the skate is absolutely fresh. There should be no doubt about this in a good bistro or brasserie, but if you are cooking it at home, give the fish a good sniff before you buy; if it smells of anything but fresh brine and sea salt, leave it on the fishmonger's slab.

SERVES 4
PREPARATION TIME: 5 MINUTES
COOKING TIME: 20 MINUTES

4 skate wings, about
    225g/8oz each
salt and freshly ground
    black pepper
4 tbsp red wine vinegar

2 tbsp capers in vinegar,
    drained
150g/5oz/⅔ cup unsalted
    butter

Put the skate in a wide shallow skillet (frying pan), cover with cold water, and add a pinch of salt and 1 tablespoon of the vinegar. Bring to a boil, remove any scum from the surface, then lower the heat and simmer for 10–12 minutes, until you can easily push the flesh away from the cartilage.

Drain the skate, carefully peel off the skin, and put the wings in a warm serving dish. Season with salt and pepper, sprinkle on the capers, and keep the skate warm.

In a small saucepan, heat the butter until it foams and turns a rich nutty brown (it should not turn black, despite the name of the dish). Pour it over the skate. Put the remaining vinegar in the pan and boil to reduce to about 1 tablespoon. Drizzle it over the skate and serve immediately.

Street markets & market streets

Food is never far from the mind of the Parisians. For them, it's a passion and when they aren't eating food, they are talking about their last meal or planning the next and deciding which ingredients to buy and where. There is certainly no lack of choice; the city boasts more street markets than anywhere else in Europe. Almost every quarter has a street market (*marché volant*) where traders set up their stands at first light on a couple of fixed days every week, moving from one area to another on different days.

Traditional Parisians still prefer to shop in open-air markets, confident of finding the finest seasonal produce, artisan charcuterie and breads, cheeses straight from the farm, aromatic herbs, and fish whose silvery scales, bright, bulging eyes, and scarlet gills attest to their freshness. Shopping in the market is a ritual and no one expects it to be like a supermarket dash. There is fruit to squeeze (on pain of incurring the market trader's wrath), the first asparagus or strawberries to savor, aromatic herbs and pungent cheeses to sniff, and recipes to discuss, along with the familiar banter between standholders and regular customers. All this takes ages, but it's a time-honored ritual that makes food shopping a treat.

The atmosphere is less frenetic in the market streets, but the range of foods on offer is superb, and the shops are open every day except Mondays. It's a joy to wander along the pedestrianized streets, where shopping is an inside-outside affair, with stalls spilling out from the shop fronts into the street, interspersed with lively cafés and bars. Each street typifies the quarter and has its own unique character. The rue Montorgueil in the 1st and 2nd arrondissements is the sole surviving remnant of the late-lamented Les Halles market. Until recently this ancient cobbled street had a grubby charm; now it has been spruced up, but retains its authentic, lively character with a terrific fish shop, an old-fashioned chocolatier, fromagerie, and Paris's oldest pâtisserie, the venerable Stohrer.

Across the river in the Latin Quarter, rue Mouffetard is one of the oldest streets in Paris and a haunt of students attracted by the cheap food on offer. The name means "smelly street" and there's a whiff of seediness about the lively daily market, which retains a medieval atmosphere, with some gruesome displays in butchers' shops, and the sounds and scents of traders selling dried fish, dusty beans, and exotic spices. Crammed between the butchers, bakers, and candlestick-makers are crêperies, fondue and raclette bistros, and the wittily named Mouff' Tartes, selling rather tasty sweet and savory tarts by the slice.

The vibrant rue de Buci, in the heart of St-Germain is a student favorite, but the produce here is neither cheap nor rough and ready. Artfully arranged stalls offer the finest cheeses, seafood, colorful fruits, and pâtisserie. The vegetables burst with freshness and the heavenly aroma from Paul's coffee shop mingles with the fragrance of the flowers outside the florist on the corner.

Parisians are fiercely proud of their neighborhood market streets. Whichever quarter you are in, the locals will assure you that *their* street offers the best range of food in Paris. Should you be visiting Montmartre, you'll find an overwhelming range of tempting comestibles in the popular rue du Poteau. If the Eiffel Tower is on your itinerary, rue Clerc has the best Italian delicatessen, and an excellent fromagerie, and a host of other upmarket food shops and eateries.

Picnicking in Paris is a joy; pick up the wherewithal in the rue de Lévis and eat with gusto in the elegant Parc Monceau, or buy an al fresco feast in the rue de l'Annonciation and head for the Bois de Boulogne with your spoils. One thing is sure — you are never far from fabulous food in Paris.

Landmarks

It may be unfair to the architect but Parisians say that you get the best views of Paris at the top of the 685-foot-high Tour Montparnasse because it's the only place from which you can't see the much-loathed tower. The original narrow streets of Montparnasse far below have been replaced with rather unattractive concrete blocks, but there is still plenty to enjoy here — apart from its multi-cultural gourmet treats. You can catch up on some reading at the fantastic Bibliothèque Nationale de France, wander around the tapestry museum, les Gobelins, or contemplate the area's luminous and artistic past at the somber but fascinating Cimetière de Montparnasse.

Bibliothèque Nationale de France

The last and most expensive of President Mitterand's Grands Projets, the French National Library opened in 1996 to general opprobrium. The 1960s-style design, whose four L-shaped towers symbolize open books, was considered dated, far too expensive and ill-conceived: the eleven million books and documents were stored in the glass towers without blinds to protect them from the sun (wooden boards have since been fitted). The central sunken so-called "Garden of Eden" was filled with 140 mature trees removed from Versailles at a cost of more than forty million euros. But Parisians have learnt to love their library. Much of it (although unfortunately not the garden) is open to the public, the research facilities are superb, and any adult can sit in the exceptionally comfortable chairs and enjoy the many books, periodicals, and newspapers. The four annual special exhibitions and classical concerts are always worth a visit.

Cimetière de Montparnasse

Montparnasse was home to so many illustrious artists, writers, and musicians that it's no surprise to find the cemetery (right) packed with their graves. Built in 1824 on the site of three farms, the huge burial ground became the last resting place of literary luminaries such as the poet Baudelaire, the playwright Samuel Beckett, Alexandre Dumas *"fils"*, the lovers Simone de Beauvoir and Jean-Paul Sartre. Artists include Brancusi, whose childlike pastiche of Rodin's *"The Kiss"* adorns a tomb in the north-eastern corner, Frédéric Bartholdi (who sculpted the Statue of Liberty), Man Ray, and Henri Langlois, founder of France's national

cinematic collection, whose unusual memorial lies smothered in small stills from great films.

Les Manufactures Nationales de Tapis et Tapisseries (les Gobelins)

An elegant set of seventeenth-century buildings on the avenue des Gobelins houses the famous tapestry factory. In the fifteenth century, Jean Gobelin founded a humble dye works on the banks of the River Bièvre. His discovery of a scarlet dye made from cochineal earned him a fortune, but turned the water red and contributed to the pollution that resulted in the river being covered over. The family turned to tapestry weaving, another hugely successful business venture. The superlative quality of their work induced Louis XIV's finance minister, Colbert, to appropriate the establishment in 1662. Using designs by the finest artists of the day, skilled weavers created a wealth of magnificent tapestries to adorn the Sun King's court. Apart from a brief interruption during the Revolution, les Gobelins has continued to manufacture tapestries up to the present day. Guided visits allow you to watch the weavers at work and admire some of the historic wall-hangings.

Tour Montparnasse

There's no doubt that the Tour Montparnasse is a typically ugly 1970s edifice, but once Europe's fastest lift has whizzed you up fifty-six floors in just thirty-eight seconds to the picture-windowed panoramic terrace, you can only marvel at the stupendous 270-degree view across the city. Like a panorama in a tourist guidebook, almost all of Paris's great landmarks are displayed before you: the Eiffel Tower, Les Invalides, the Arc de Triomphe, the Louvre, Notre-Dame, and beyond. It's even

more magical at night, when the lights of the brightly illuminated boulevards stretch out like twinkling moonbeams. Relax with a coffee in the panoramic café-lounge, or steel yourself to climb three flights of stairs to the breezy open-air terrace on the fifty-ninth floor for an unobscured 360-degree view of the city.

Pipérade

Scrambled eggs with tomatoes and bell peppers

Brunch is a comparatively new concept for Parisians, but they have embraced the idea with enthusiasm and many brasseries and restaurants now serve weekend brunches, with dishes like this featuring on the menu. Pipérade is normally served hot, but it is equally good cold and makes a great light lunch or brunch.

SERVES 4
PREPARATION TIME: 10 MINUTES
COOKING TIME: ABOUT 20 MINUTES

8 very ripe tomatoes
3 tbsp olive oil
2 onions, peeled and diced
275g/10oz red bell peppers, seeded and finely diced
2 garlic cloves, finely chopped
8 large eggs
salt and freshly ground black pepper

Fill a large bowl with boiling water, cut a small cross in the skin of each tomato, and drop them into the water. Remove and drain after 1 minute, and peel the skin off the tomatoes. Cut the peeled tomatoes into quarters, remove and discard the seeds, then dice the flesh.

Heat 2 tablespoons of the olive oil in a skillet (frying pan) set over a medium heat, add the onions, and sweat them for about 5 minutes to soften but not color them. Add the bell peppers and garlic and cook gently for another 5 minutes. Add the tomatoes and cook until the juices have evaporated.

Break the eggs into a bowl, season with salt and pepper, and beat lightly with a fork. Pour them into the skillet and scramble the eggs over a low heat, bringing the edges into the middle as they begin to set. Just before they reach the consistency you prefer, stir in the remaining olive oil. Serve the pipérade on warm plates with good country bread.

Crème Brûlée

Crème brûlée is a perennial favorite which needs little enhancement, but in summer you might like to make a layer of raspberries or wild strawberries in the bottom of the dishes for a delightful surprise when you dig into the baked cream.

SERVES 6
PREPARATION TIME: 10 MINUTES
COOKING TIME: 35–45 MINUTES, PLUS 1 HOUR CHILLING

510ml/18fl oz/2 cups heavy (double) cream
1 vanilla bean (pod), split lengthwise
2 tbsp superfine (caster) sugar
4 large egg yolks
75g/3oz/¼ cup packed soft dark brown or demerara sugar

Preheat the oven to 170°C/325°F/ gas mark 3. Pour the cream into a small saucepan. Scrape in the seeds from the vanilla bean using a knife tip. Add the vanilla bean to the pan and gently heat the cream until it just begins to bubble at the edge. Put the 4 egg yolks and superfine sugar in a bowl and whisk lightly until pale and slightly thickened. When the cream starts to bubble, remove the vanilla bean and pour the cream into the egg yolks, whisking as you go.

Arrange six ramekins or gratin dishes in a roasting pan and ladle in the custard mixture. Pour enough boiling water into the pan to come halfway up the sides of the ramekins or dishes.

Bake in the oven for 30–40 minutes until the custard is just set but still trembling. Put the dishes on a wire rack to cool, then chill for at least 1 hour.

Sprinkle the dark brown or demerara sugar evenly over the custards and caramelize with a cook's blowtorch until crusty, or place under a very hot broiler (grill) until the sugar has caramelized, taking care that it does not burn.

Pages 200–1: a typical busy weekday scene in the Montparnasse area.

Glossary

Affineur(se): A skilled cheese expert who buys young cheeses and stores and ripens them to perfect maturity.

Amuse-bouche: Appetizer, designed to awaken the taste buds. Also known as *amuse-gueule*.

Ancienne cuisine: Classic, complex French cooking, using traditional methods that require a high degree of technical skill and training.

Andouillette: Pork sausage made from pig's intestines. Usually grilled and served hot with mustard.

Art deco: Highly decorative style of 1920–30, featuring geometric patterns and bright colors.

Art nouveau: "New art" evolved in the late nineteenth century, that was inspired by organic shapes taken from nature.

Bake blind: Initial baking of a pastry case without its filling (sweet or savory) to prevent the filling making the pastry soggy.

Ballottine: Boned, rolled and stuffed poultry or meat. Foie gras or mousse rolled into a cylindrical shape.

Banc: A counter on which foods are displayed.

Batterie de cuisine: Kitchen utensils and equipment.

Belle Epoque: Literally "beautiful era". The period in French history from 1890 until World War I. It was considered to be a time of technological innovation and peace. Belle-époque brasseries retain their lavish décor.

Biologique: Organic.

Brik: North African filo-pasty turnover filled with fish, meat, cheese, spinach, or a whole egg and deep-fried. *Borek* is similar and variations are found in Sephardi Jewish cooking.

Bouchon: Literally "cork". Denotes a modest bistro/bar serving simple food and wine.

Boudin blanc: Smooth sausage of white meats like pork, veal, and poultry.

Boudin noir: Blood sausage.

Boulangerie: Bakery.

Bouquet garni: A bundle of herbs (classically thyme, bay leaf, and parsley) tied with string and used to flavor dishes. It is removed before serving.

Bouillabaisse: Provençal stew-like fish soup. Typically contains *rascasse* (scorpion fish), conger eel, plus other Mediterranean fish and seafood.

B'stilla (also pastilla): Fragrant North African pie topped with layers of wafer-thin pastry sprinkled with cinnamon and sugar, contrasting with a savory filling like pigeon, chicken, or rabbit.

Beurre manié: Equal quantities of flour and softened butter mixed to make a thickening agent for sauces.

Cassoulet: A robust slow-cooked stew, originally from Toulouse, with haricot beans, pork, sausages, and confit meats like duck or goose.

Charcuterie: Prepared and cooked meats (originally exclusively pork), including hams, sausages, terrines, and pâtés. Also a pork butcher, or a delicatessen selling cooked meats and pork products.

Chaussons: Pastry-wrapped turnovers.

Chèvre: Literally "goat", but can also denote goat's cheese.

Chocolatier: Chocolate-maker. The best are maître-chocolatiers (master chocolate makers).

Choucroûte: Alasatian dish of sauerkraut (pickled fermented cabbage). Choucroûte garni is served hot with sausages, pork and other meats.

Civet: Rich game stew (usually hare or venison) thickened with the animal's blood.

Confit: Poultry (usually duck and goose), meat or game slow-cooked and preserved in its own fat, or in pork fat. May also be used to denote candied or crystalized fruits.

Coq au vin: Traditionally rooster (now any mature fowl) stewed in robust red wine with button onions, bacon, and mushrooms until very tender.

Crème anglaise: Fresh egg custard made to a pouring consistency.

Crème pâtissière: Pastry cream.

Cru: Raw, as in crudités, or to refer to wine growth. Fine wines are classified into *grands crus* (great growths), *premiers crus* (first growths), etc.

Dégustation: Tasting (such as wines or cheeses). A *menu dégustation* has several small dishes using seasonal ingredients, designed to showcase the chef's talents.

Epoisses: Cheese from Burgundy. The rind is washed with *marc de Bourgogne* as it matures.

Délice: Light dessert or small moussey cake.

Fin-de-siècle: Literally "end of the century". Implies decadence and luxury.

Fleur de sel: The finest flakes of sea salt.

Fougasse: Plaited or shaped flat bread originally baked on the hearth embers.

Fruits de mer: An assortment of shellfish and crustaceans. A *plateau de fruits de mer* consists of raw and cooked oysters, clams, and whelks plus crab, langoustines, and sometimes lobster piled on crushed ice and served with shallot vinegar and mayonnaise.

Gigot: Leg of lamb, poultry, or monkfish tail shaped and tied to resemble a leg of lamb.

Glacier: Ice cream and sorbet maker and/or seller.

Haute cuisine: Refined cooking based on classical techniques in the finest French tradition.

Hôtels particuliers: Grand private houses or mansions.

Jus: Cooking juices from roast or pan-fried meat, used as a very pure gravy.

Langoustines: Scampi or Dublin Bay prawn.

Lardons: Small squares or batons of bacon.

Maître-fromager: Master cheesemaker.

Magret: Boneless duck breast, originally from force-fed ducks used for foie gras. Nowadays used to describe any large duck breast fillet.

Marché volant: Roving street market.

Marrons glacés: Candied sweet chestnuts.

Moelleux au chocolat: Light baked chocolate pudding with a liquid chocolate centre.

Nouvelle cuisine: A lighter, more refined modern way of cooking, developed in the 1970s as a reaction to rich, heavy, traditional cuisine. Presentation became as important as the food and portions were small but decorative. Often misinterpreted and usually over-priced, its popularity declined within twenty years.

Pain d'épices: Spiced gingerbread-like cake, reputedly brought to France by the Crusaders.

Palmiers: Sweet glazed puff-pastry cookies shaped like a palm leaf.

Pavé: Literally "cobblestone". Denotes square-shaped foods like cheeses, cakes, or thick-cut fillets of beef or veal.

Petit salé: Lightly salted pork belly.

Plat du jour: Dish of the day.

Poissonnerie: Fresh fish and seafood shop.

Pommes mousseline: Very light puréed potatoes.

Pommes à la vapeur: Boiled or steamed potatoes.

Pot-au-feu: Traditional one-pot dish of boiled beef, root vegetables, and broth.

Prix fixe: Set-price menu.

Quenelles: Very light poached fish or chicken mousse, typically *de brochet* (pike). Usually oval-shaped.

Rascasse: Scorpion fish, an essential ingredient of authentic *bouillabaisse*.

Ras-el-hanout: An aromatic Moroccan blend of up to fifteen spices, including ginger, cardamom, cinnamon, coriander, allspice, nutmeg, and dried rosebuds.

Rémoulade: Mayonnaise sharpened with mustard, capers, cornichons, and chopped herbs. Served with cold meat and fish, and often mixed with shredded celeriac.

Rillettes: Shredded cooked meat (usually pork) potted in its own fat.

Rôtisseur: One who spit-roasts meat and poultry, often including suckling pig.

Rue commerçante: Market street.

Sablés: Crumbly sweet cookies, similar to fine shortbread.

Savarin: Yeast cake, often baked in an elaborate fluted ring mould and soaked in kirsch or rum (for a rum baba).

Soupe à l'oignon gratinée: Classic lyonnais onion soup poured over a thick slice of baguette, topped with grated Gruyère, and browned.

Steak tartare: Raw finely chopped beef steak mixed with raw egg yolk, onions, and capers.

Syndicat d'Initiative: Tourist Information Office.

Table d'hôte: Set fixed-price menu of two or more courses.

Tablier de sapeur: Literally "fireman's apron". A lyonnais dish of grilled breaded tripe.

Tartare: Very finely chopped raw beef or fish. *Sauce tartare* is mayonnaise with capers, cornichons, mustard, and chopped onion.

Tomme de Savoie: A large, sweet, mild cheese from Savoie, made from partially skimmed milk. Tomme is the Savoyard patois for "cheese".

Traiteur: Purveyor selling ready-prepared dishes (tarts, pies, salads, terrines, casseroles, etc).

Vacherin: Meringue dessert filled with whipped cream, fruit, ice cream, etc. Also a delicious creamy Alpine cheese, with a center so runny that it can be eaten with a spoon.

Viennoiserie: Viennese pastries and any baked goods other than bread, and cookies such as croissants, brioches, macaroons, and sablés.

Volaille de Bresse: Free-range poultry from Bresse raised under strict controls, including diet (corn and buckwheat), genetic purity, and from within a strictly defined geographic area. Bresse chickens have white feathers and delicate white flesh and blue legs, and are considered to be the best poultry in France.

Index

Acknowledgments

Abbreviations for terms appearing below: (t) top; (b) bottom; (c) center; (l) left; (r) right; (AA) AA World Travel Library.

The Automobile Association wishes to thank the following photographers, companies and picture agencies for their assistance in the preparation of this book.

3l Peter Cassidy/ABPL; 3cl AA/J Tims; 3cr AA/C Sawyer; 3r AA/M Jourdan; 5t AA/K Paterson; 5ct AA/M Jourdan; 5c AA/C Sawyer; 5cb J Billic/Photocuisine UK; 5b AA/W Voysey; 7AA/C Sawyer; 8-9 AA/P Enticknap; 11t AA/B Rieger; 11ct AA/C Sawyer; 11c AA/C Sawyer; 11cb AA/C Sawyer; 11b AA/C Sawyer; 12 & 13 AA/C Sawyer; 14-15 AA/B Rieger; 16 AA/M Jourdan; 17ct AA/C Sawyer; 17ctc, 17c, 17cbc AA/T Souter; 17cb AA/B Rieger; 18 & 19 AA/C Sawyer; 20-21 AA/K Paterson; 22 AA/C Sawyer; 23 AA/T Souter; 24 Y Bagros/Photocuisine UK; 26 & 27 AA/C Sawyer; 28 AA; 31 J Billic/Photocuisine UK; 32tl AA/P Enticknap; 32b AA/P Kenward; 33 AA/T Souter; 34-35 AA/P Kenward; 36 AA/K Paterson; 37ct AA/M Jourdan; 37ctc AA/T Souter; 37c AA/K Paterson; 37cbc AA/C Sawyer; 37cb AA/K Paterson; 38 AA/C Sawyer; 39 AA/B Smith; 40-41 AA/C Sawyer; 42-43 AA/B Rieger; 45 Foodpix/Photolibrary; 46 AA/C Sawyer; 47bl AA/K Paterson; 47tr AA/C Sawyer; 49 Peter Cassidy/ABPL; 50 AA/C Sawyer; 52tl AA/K Paterson; 52b AA/T Souter; 53 - 55 AA/C Sawyer; 56 AA/M Jourdan; 57 AA/C Sawyer; 58 AA/B Rieger; 59-61 AA/C Sawyer; 62bl AA/C Sawyer; 62tr AA/K Paterson; 63 AA/C Sawyer; 65 AA/B Rieger; 67 Tim Imrie/ABPL; 68 Ritz Escoffier Cooking School; 70 Foodpix/Photolibrary; 72 AA/M Jourdan; 73 AA/B Rieger; 74-75 AA/K Paterson; 76-77 AA/J Tims; 78 AA/M Jourdan; 79ct AA/C Sawyer; 79ctc AA/T Souter; 79c AA/M Jourdan; 79cbc AA/C Sawyer; 79cb AA/B Rieger; 80-81 AA/C Sawyer; 82-83 AA/M Joudan; 84-86 AA/C Sawyer; 87 AA/M Short; 89 Foodpix/Photolibrary; 90-91 AA/B Rieger; 93 Jean Cazals; 94-95 AA/M Jourdan; 96-97 AA/J Tims; 98-99 AA/K Paterson; 100 AA/P Kenward; 101-102 AA/C Sawyer; 103tl AA/M Short; 103br AA/C Sawyer; 104-106 AA/C Sawyer; 107tr AA/B Rieger; 107bl AA/M Short; 108 AA/S McBride; 109 AA/C Sawyer; 110 Y Bagros/Photocuisine UK; 112tl AA/K Paterson; 112b AA/C Sawyer; 113 AA/J Tims; 114-115 AA/M Jourdan; 117 Jean Cazals; 118-119 AA/C Sawyer; 120 AA/T Souter; 121t AA/M Jourdan; 121ct AA/M Jourdan; 121c AA/M Jourdan; 121cb AA/C Sawyer; 121b AA/K Paterson; 122 AA/C Sawyer; 123t AA/C Sawyer; 123b Photodisc; 124 AA/B Rieger; 125 AA/C Sawyer; 126 AA/M Jourdan; 127t AA/C Sawyer; 127b Bel Canto; 129 Steve Lee/ABPL; 130-131 AA/M Jourdan; 132 Steve Lee/ABPL; 134t AA/K Paterson; 134b AA/M Jourdan; 135 AA/C Sawyer; 137 J Billic/Photocuisine UK; 138-139 AA/W Voysey; 140-141 AA/J Tims; 142 & 143tc AA/B Rieger; 143tr AA/C Sawyer; 143c AA/C Sawyer; 143cr AA/M Jourdan; 144 AA/C Sawyer; 145 AA/C Sawyer; 146 Premium/ABPL; 147 AA/C Sawyer; 149 J Billic/Photocuisine UK; 150 AA/E Ellington; 151 AA/C Sawyer; 153 Martin Brigdale/ABPL; 154t AA/P Enticknap; 154b AA/K Paterson; 155 AA/M Jourdan; 157 Foodpix/Photolibrary; 158-159 AA/T Souter; 160-161 AA/J Tims; 162 AA/C Sawyer; 163tc AA/M Jourdan; 163tr AA/T Souter; 163c & 163cr AA/K Paterson; 164 Berthillon; 165t AA/C Sawyer; 165b AA/T Souter; 166-167 AA/P Enticknap; 168 AA/C Sawyer; 169t AA/M Jourdan; 169b & 170–173 AA/C Sawyer; 175 Christian Adam/Photocuisine UK; 176t AA/C Sawyer; 176b AA/M Jourdan; 177 AA/M Jourdan; 178 Y Bagros/Photocuisine UK; 180-188 AA/C Sawyer; 189 & 190 AA/B Rieger; 191 AA/C Sawyer; 193 Tim Hill/ABPL; 194-197 AA/C Sawyer; 199 Jean Cazals; 200-201 AA/M Jourdan; 203t AA/C Sawyer; 203ct Jean Cazals; 203c, 203cb & 203b AA/C Sawyer; 205t AA/M Jourdan; 205ct AA/M Jourdan; 205c, 205cb & 205b AA/C Sawyer; 207t AA/T Souter; 207ct AA/W Voysey; 207c AA/M Jourdan; 207cb AA/M Jourdan; 207b AA/C Sawyer.

Every effort has been made to trace the copyright holders, and we apologise in advance for any accidental errors. We would be happy to apply the corrections in the following edition of this publication.